The Miracle Ministry of the Prophet

The Miracle Ministry of the Prophet

Dr. Christian Harfouche

Power House Publishers
Pensacola, Florida

The Miracle Ministry of the Prophet
Published by:
Power House Publishers
2411 Executive Plaza Road
Pensacola, FL 32504
ISBN 0-9634451-5-4
www.globalrevival.com

Second Printing, June 2000

Cover design and book production by:
DB & Associates Design & Distribution
dba Double Blessing Productions
P.O. Box 52756, Tulsa, OK 74152
www.doubleblessing.com

Editorial Consultant: Phyllis Mackall, Broken Arrow, Oklahoma

Printed in the United States of America.

Contents

Introduction

Paul said to the Roman church, "I long to see you, that I may impart unto you some spiritual gift, to the end ye might be established" (Romans 1:11).

It is my desire to teach you by the anointing of the Holy Spirit so revelation would impart and trigger in you the supernatural abilities God has already given you through the Spirit.

It is my conviction that what Jesus accomplished in His ministry is the absolute limit. We can never surpass Jesus' standard, but we can definitely press into what He had in His life and ministry.

Although the disciple is not above his master (Matthew 10:24,25), as believers we are called to do *greater works* through faith in Him. It is His victory on Calvary that provided our authority. We can come to the fullness of Christ (Ephesians 4:13). He is the standard for perfection.

Jesus said if what we do is the result of our faith in Him, we will do the same works — not words — that He did. Then He went on to say, "...and *greater* works than these shall he do, because I go unto my Father" (John 14:12).

It was Jude who wrote in verse 3 that believers "should earnestly contend for the faith which was once delivered unto the saints."

Today, in this liberal, double-minded decade, we need to contend earnestly for the God-kind of faith — not the religious form of faith, and not man's opinion of faith — but biblical faith.

Without faith it is impossible to please God, and without faith, everything we do is dead. Dead works will not benefit anyone; but faith works will empty a hospital room, raise a person from the dead, and open blind eyes. Faith works will trigger the power necessary to override impossible circumstances.

Would you like to see the impossibilities in your life turn around because you, by an act of your will, are able to biblically trigger the power of God that is resident in you? Of course you would.

That's why I want to pour into your heart, confirm, and validate what God has already put within you. Then you can begin to rise to a level of faith where the manifestation of that invisible faith will become *visible*.

In other words, the devil will obey when you command him; the disease will leave when you talk to it; the situation will turn around when you confront it — because you've got active faith living in you!

— *Christian Harfouche*

The Miracle Ministry of the Prophet

Chapter 1
The Missing Art of Imparting

If there is a missing art in the Church today, it is the art of imparting, transmitting, and receiving the same kind of faith Jesus left with the apostles two thousand years ago.

I believe God has given the fivefold ministry gifts the ability to impart the same kind of ministry power they possess to others.

The anointing can be transmitted through them to others in the Body of Christ so the Church may be successful in doing what God has called it to do.

Jesus said, "My joy I give unto you." He said, "I give you my name. In my name you are going to do these things." And He said, "I am going to leave my Word with you."

By saying these things, Jesus left the Church with an awareness of what the Christ-kind of ministry would be. The Holy Spirit came to endorse and enforce that ministry and to help the Church walk miraculously in the midst of a world that is bound, is natural in its outlook, and bows its knee to impossibility.

Hebrews 1:9 says about Jesus:

Thou hast loved righteousness, and hated iniquity; therefore God, even thy God, hath anointed thee with the oil of gladness above thy fellows.

The moment you love the Word of God and the things of God and hate things that are not righteousness, certain changes take place in you. For example, you develop *discernment*, which is the ability to detect between right and wrong.

1

Then, because you loved righteousness so much once you learned what it is, the Father will anoint you with the oil of gladness the way He anointed Jesus. As we just read in Hebrews 1:9, "...therefore God, even thy God, hath anointed thee...." Have you wondered why certain vessels are more anointed than others?

I believe with all my heart that there is a certain level of unction, or anointing, that cannot come without the love of righteousness and the hatred of iniquity.

Yes, everyone who is full of the Holy Spirit has a certain measure of anointing, and everyone who is called into the fivefold ministry has a higher level of endowment or anointing.

Pressing in to the Great Miracles

However, it is only those who have developed a hunger for righteousness who are able to press into the great miracles, the earth-shaking miracles, the kind of lifestyle in God that can validate and demonstrate that you are not alone; that God is with you.

So let us develop an awareness of the different levels of anointing that are available to us.

In Luke 4, we read that Jesus visited the synagogue at Nazareth one Sabbath and said:

The Spirit of the Lord is upon me, because he hath anointed me to preach the gospel to the poor; he hath sent me to heal the brokenhearted, to preach deliverance to the captives, and recovering of sight to the blind, to set at liberty them that are bruised,

To preach the acceptable year of the Lord.

And he closed the book, and he gave it again to the minister, and sat down. And the eyes of all of them that were in the synagogue were fastened on him.

And he began to say unto them, This day is this scripture fulfilled in your ears.

Luke 4:18-21

The Mantle of a Pioneer

I want to point out something here about the ministry of the prophet, or the individual who brings a word that is a *rhema* — a word that is active, challenging, and dominating at the time.

Anyone who brings a word that says, "*Now* is the time for your miracle; *now* is the time for your deliverance; *now* is the time for revival" has, in essence, put on the mantle of a pioneer.

Such a person is not going to put up with the status quo; he is going to speak what God gives him, telling the truth in spite of the danger of its hurting someone's feelings. Jesus came with that same attitude to the synagogue. Why? Because He was anointed by the Holy Spirit!

When you are under the influence of the Holy Spirit, you are not afraid of the bondage of men, because you know you have sufficient power to transform, change, and deliver. And you know who you are.

Jesus did not make any pretense about the fact that the Spirit of the Lord was upon Him. Someone will say, "Well, that was Jesus." However, Jesus had been baptized in water only a short time before.

He had never made that claim before the Spirit of the Lord came upon Him and anointed him at the River Jordan. He had never made that claim until He was tested in the wilderness and He resisted the devil through the written Word, saying, "It is written...it is written...it is written." He had never made that claim until He returned in the Spirit and the power of God.

When He returned with that anointing and entered the synagogue, it was not a pretense. He just walked in and zeroed in on the appropriate scripture for the day.

The Prophetic Life

Your life today is a prophetic life. Your life today is a *rhema* life. It tells everyone you are serving a *living* God, not a dead God, not a God who used to do it, but a God who is doing it today! Your life should have that "air" about it because of the anointing that is upon you through the Holy Spirit.

When Jesus came into the synagogue, He said (and I'm paraphrasing), "I know that heaven has been silent for hundreds of years. I know that since Malachi until now you have not seen a move of God, but here is Isaiah 61:1, and I'm quoting it to you:

"The Spirit of the Lord is upon Me, because He has anointed Me to do these things. I am going to heal the brokenhearted, preach recovering of sight to the blind. I am going to bring a miracle move, because I am going to preach the acceptable year of the Lord — the Jubilee Year — the year where God is active, the year and the hour where man no longer needs to wait for a future date in God."

Anytime you make such a bold proclamation, there are many who will not readily receive you; however, those who are hungry will. Those who are not ready for change, those who are mindful of their excuses more than they are of the antidote, will not readily receive you. Their excuses will keep them out of God's best for their life.

Here comes Jesus in Bible days, who says, "It's time for change!" Here comes any believer today who believes in signs and wonders, who believes that the Holy Spirit is active today, who believes that the Word of God is alive in them and with them. They have an air about them — an attitude about them — because they cannot stand to leave things the way they are. They want to change things because they know it is possible with God; because they know they are anointed by God to do it.

The Pharisees' Question

The Pharisees who were present in the synagogue that day immediately had a question, because this was Nazareth, after all, and they were accustomed to seeing Jesus the way

4

He used to be — before His baptism with the Holy Spirit and before His commitment to ministry.

In essence, His commitment was a decision whereby He said, "Whenever I meet a devil, I'm going to defeat it. Whenever I meet a disease or some other need, I'm going to meet it. I'm not going to trespass over people's wills, but whenever I'm invited, I will meet the need." That was Jesus' decision.

You are going to have to make a similar decision. The devil will tempt you to go back on this decision, and people who are accustomed to the way you used to be are going to challenge you once they begin to see you in a new light, now that you are audacious, bold, and quite different in your conduct. They are going to ask you the same question the Pharisees asked Jesus: *"Who do you think you are?"*

After Jesus came down off the mountain where He was tempted, the people of His hometown were shocked, because the man who stood before them that Sabbath, reading that scripture, had a completely different disposition than the man they were used to. So they started wondering about Him.

Jesus' Reply

Jesus' reply reveals one of the hindrances to a miracle ministry and how to overcome it. He replied starting in verse 23:

Ye will surely say unto me this proverb, Physician, heal thyself: whatsoever we have heard done in Capernaum, do also here in thy country.

And he said, Verily I say unto you, No prophet is accepted in his own country.

But I tell you of a truth, many widows were in Israel in the days of Elias, when the heaven was shut up three years and six months, when great famine was throughout all the land;

But unto none of them was Elias sent, save unto Sarepta, a city of Sidon, unto a woman that was a widow.

5

And many lepers were in Israel in the time of Eliseus the prophet; and none of them was cleansed, saving Naaman the Syrian.

And all they in the synagogue, when they heard these things, were filled with wrath,

And rose up, and thrust him out of the city, and led him unto the brow of the hill whereon their city was built, that they might cast him down headlong.

Luke 4:23-29

Jesus returned to Nazareth with the miracle power of God! He was bold to declare change as He said, "This is the year the Lord has made. I have come to preach the acceptable year of the Lord. I have the power that is needed to do it. The Spirit of the Lord is upon Me."

When He detected an attitude in the hearts of the people, He didn't remain silent about it or preach over it. He immediately said, "You would say to Me..." In other words, "You'd like to tell Me, 'Physician, heal yourself. What we hear You're doing in other towns, do also here in your hometown.'"

Why were they thinking that? Because their attitude was, "If we see Him do it, we'll believe it. You want us to believe it; do it."

Attitude Fights Gift

Jesus immediately resisted; a man of God will resist that type of spirit. Jesus learned to detect it because it clashed against the miracle gift God had put on His life!

So Jesus immediately said to them, "This is what your attitude is, but I'll tell you of a truth: In the days of the prophets there were many widows in Israel, but the prophet Elijah wasn't sent to one of them. In the days of Elisha, there were many lepers in Israel, but only Naaman the Syrian was healed."

We can see by what Jesus said that only one widow and only one leper were ready to believe in an instantaneous change through a visitation from God. That's why God never sent His prophets to heal any of the others: They were not ready to believe in an instantaneous change!

Deadened by Skepticism

Why is it that the Church today by and large has lost its edge to convert sinners, to cast out the devil, to break the power of drug addiction, and to bring a miracle-working cure that is greater in its dimensions than the medical community can accomplish?

It is because the Church has been resisted by the mentality and the thoughts of skeptics, who say, "We've heard it was done in Bible days. Now do it here that we might believe it."

Jesus' response to that attitude was, "Don't worry about it; you won't get the power, the invasion, the healing, or the breakthrough in your life if your attitude is that of a skeptic."

Chapter 2
Children of Destiny

Some people think this matter of healing the sick and believing in the supernatural, prosperity, and casting out devils is a new thing. I want to show you it isn't.

Let's look back at just one hundred years of Church history. We find that for a long time there *was* a voice; God used many men and women in operating the gifts of the Holy Spirit during the last century — more, in fact, than we could ever study during this brief time.

However, I have chosen several who I believe are fascinating because they seemed to know exactly where they were going in God. They had a spirit of boldness about them.

When they came on the scene, it was as if a voice — the thundering voice of a prophet — said, "World, you may not be ready for this, but here I am with God — and we're not going to let things continue the way they are!"

These men and women were children of destiny!

John Alexander Dowie: Apostle of Healing

The first such person we are going to study is *John Alexander Dowie.* His name may be all but forgotten today, but he was known to millions at the turn of the century, some with respect and some with derision.

Dowie started as just a normal clergyman. He was pastoring a Congregational church in a suburb of Sydney when a plague suddenly hit Australia, and people started dying by the thousands, including some members of his congregation.

Until this time, Dowie had been a traditional clergyman. He had never prayed for the sick with faith, and he had never seen a miracle. But now his flock needed miracles. His heart especially broke over three little children in his congregation who were dying.

At that time the commonly held belief was that God puts sickness and disease on people. "Does God put sickness on innocent little children?" Dowie asked himself. "Does He snatch their parents from them, leaving them helpless orphans?" he wondered. The devastating plague drove Dowie to search the scriptures for answers.

Dowie's Revelation of Divine Healing

John Alexander Dowie received the revelation he sought from Acts 10:38:

How God anointed Jesus of Nazareth with the Holy Ghost and with power: *who went about doing good, and healing all that were oppressed of the devil:* **for God was with him.**

This one scripture exploded in Dowie's consciousness, forever changing his life and, ultimately, the lives of millions of others around the world.

Dowie's quest and revelation took him to other healing scriptures. He read that "Jesus Christ [is] the same yesterday, and to day, and for ever" (Hebrews 13:8). He found that Jesus took our infirmities, carried our diseases, and gave us power over darkness — and by His stripes we were healed.

And Dowie prayed the prayer of faith with such success that not one of his flock died in the epidemic after he received this revelation, and the three sick children were healed. He covered that church with God's power during the time when the plague was running throughout Australia.

Dowie Tackles Chicago

In 1888, virtually unknown, Dowie came to the United States, landing first in San Francisco and later making his way to Chicago. Once established there, he fearlessly took on the religious world.

He started addressing a backslidden, lukewarm, tobacco-smoking, alcohol-drinking church, pinpointing the error of their ways just as Elijah had stood up and challenged the nation of Israel when he thought he was the only prophet alive.

There's something about taking up your responsibility in God that makes you feel important. Some people don't feel they're important, and it's because they're not doing anything worth feeling important about!

The moment you realize there is a job that will never be done unless you are involved, you will begin to find there is a destiny for you. Then God can begin to reveal to you step by step where you fit into His plans for His kingdom.

Man With a Mission

John Alexander Dowie was a man with a mission. He came heralding a message of change to a people who did not know the living God, and he was persecuted.

Dowie and his message literally shook the church world! Many religious people in Dowie's day hated him with the same ferocity that the religious people in Jesus' day hated Him.

Why? Anytime men and women of God denounce sin and call for righteousness, hate the devil and challenge people to change, the the world will try to destroy them, just like the people of Nazareth tried to destroy Jesus. They took Jesus to the brow of a hill, seeking to push Him to His death, because He had said, "Change is available for you today through Me."

So Dowie was fiercely persecuted by a hostile press as well as clergymen, city officials, lawyers, and the sellers of tobacco and liquor. He was illegally arrested many times for praying for the sick.

Arrested 100 Times!

In fact, in one year alone, he was arrested a hundred times. Sometimes he was charged with "practicing medicine without a license."

Instead of hiring a lawyer for his many court cases, Dowie trusted God to give him the wisdom to be his own trial lawyer. And if he failed in the lower courts because those courts were corrupt, he took his case to higher courts and won.

Dowie didn't mind the lawsuits at all; in fact, he seemed to *thrive* on persecution! Those who fought him ultimately disappeared from the scene or ended up dead or discredited.

So Dowie won the cases and succeeded in bringing the masses to a knowledge of the Gospel of divine healing! One of his first outreaches was to establish several Divine Healing Homes in former rooming houses in Chicago.

There the sick and the terminally ill were taught the Word of God so their faith could get to a level where they could receive their miracle. Thousands went through those healing homes.

Dowie challenged the sick with the Word of the living God and an absolute message of divine healing he believed was the only alternative for the world and medical science. And thousands of those terminally ill "guests" (never "patients"), instead of dying when their doctors predicted, recovered and lived victorious Christian lives, testifying about their miraculous healings.

Dowie had a revelation from the Word of God, and he was willing to challenge the world and bring change to it. He had a powerful healing ministry, and was especially successful in seeing people healed from malignant diseases like cancer. He once ripped a cancerous growth off a person's face with his bare hand — and the congregation then witnessed new skin appear over the wound!

Drug Addict Healed

Dr. Lilian B. Yeomans, a physician, came from a family of physicians. She was a born-again Christian who was to find that she was really a lukewarm Christian.

Because of the stress of her job, Dr. Yeomans started using a little morphine to sooth her nerves and help her get to sleep at night. After a while, to her shock and surprise, she realized that the morphine had her bound, and she was addicted to it!

Her weight dropped below 100 pounds. Her nurse described her as "a skeleton with a devil inside." Although that was not a complimentary description, she later wrote that it was true of what she had become.

When Dr. Yeomans came to John Alexander Dowie for prayer, he refused to pray for her until she had stopped taking morphine for a while. That was a strict rule of his: Dowie demanded that those who came for prayer got rid of their drugs immediately before he would pray for them.

Desperate for a Miracle

Some people have become so accustomed to a drug or a natural cure that their problem becomes less real to them, and they don't press in with desperation for God's answer.

I'm not going to argue for or against medicine. I just want to give you a little background on what these men and women of faith believed. Although you and I might think that some of them were not perfect, they achieved more than most of us put together!

Let us determine to press in to that greater dimension; to the place God has called us to walk.

When Dowie first refused to pray for Dr. Yeomans, she had to go off the morphine. Withdrawal from the drug produced severe physical problems which overwhelmed her, and she realized she needed a miracle; only God could deliver her from morphine. She later testified that she was healed in one of Dowie's Healing Homes.

Dr. Yeomans became a powerful writer for the Gospel of truth, telling about the power of God to heal. One of her best-known books is entitled *Healing From Heaven.*

Dowie's Prophetic Insight

Dr. Dowie had a prophetic insight that was more remarkable than any other preacher alive in his day. He preached and prophesied things that did not come to pass until years later.

For example, he prophesied the invention of radio during a meeting in Chicago on September 5, 1897, predicting that there would be an instrument that would enable man's voice to be carried to different cities and regions of the earth.

He also prophesied the invention of television on October 16, 1904! In the middle of a sermon, he remarked:

I know not the possibilities of electricity. It is possible that it may yet convey the face of the speaker, and, by photo-electricity, show the man as he is talking. Perhaps a discourse delivered here may be heard in every city of the United States. Some day that will be so and the word spoken in Shiloh Tabernacle will be heard even in the farthest corners of the earth.

That's prophetic insight!

We have proof that John Alexander Dowie did not speak with other tongues. I don't know what your belief is on this, but I believe in being filled with the Holy Spirit with the evidence of speaking with other tongues. However, this man was full of the Word, and he had a revelation of the healing portions of the Word.

Commitment Leads to Boldness

Dowie believed to the point of action, and he was willing to allow it to give him boldness to pray for terminally ill people and see them delivered.

Dowie had such an embrace and conviction of the Word, it gave him prophetic insight, in spite of the fact that he may not have been on the same level of blessing that you and I, who have been filled with power from on high, are on today.

The Bible says, "The steps of a good man are ordered by the Lord" (Psalm 37:23). There have been men and women in history who have performed greater miracles *without* the baptism in the Holy Spirit than some Charismatic people do *with* the baptism. Why? Because they were so committed to a measure of the Gospel, it moved them to action. If a portion is all you have, it's more than enough to bring about revival!

Today, we have better spiritual provisions. We can mix both the anointing of God and His Word; and the baptism in the Holy Spirit and the Word of God. Thus, in this decade of the '90s, our results can eclipse anyone else's in Church history. This final generation is going to see it!

The Prophetic Edge

When John Alexander Dowie, with his long white beard, stood behind his pulpit, he preached against sin and unrighteousness. In the background, mounted around the walls of the church, were crutches, canes, braces, casts, wheelchairs, and so forth that had been discarded by the joyous people who had been healed.

Dowie was the perfect picture of what a modern prophet should be like. Why? Because the moment you believe in change, in results, and in an immediate answer, you've stepped into a prophetic edge.

"If any man speaks," the Bible says, "let him speak as the oracles of God" (1 Peter 4:11). Do you know that "any man" means *you*? Whether you're called to be a prophet or not, "any man" means you. It means you can speak as the oracles of God.

Be the Antidote

In other words, there can be a prophetic edge — a *rhema* edge, a "now" word — for every circumstance you encounter, because you're utilizing the anointing God gave you to be the antidote to the situation.

Are you willing to do this? Are you willing to say, "I'm not going to yield to the status quo and be one of the majority that says there's nothing we can do about it.

"I'm going to be a messenger sent from God with the living Word, with an anointing from the Holy Spirit, and I'm going to say, 'Here we are! We are ready to see change, church growth, revival, salvation, and healing.'"

Anytime you do that, you begin to resemble a person from another world, because you are stepping into an edge where a pioneer, a prophet, a mouthpiece for God, functions. When you get into that realm — which you can with a simple decision — the Holy Spirit can work with you.

The Lord Will Work With You

When Jesus ascended and sat down at the right hand of the Father, the Bible says, "They [the disciples] went preaching every where, the Lord also working with them and confirming the word *with signs following.*"

Lay hands on yourself and say, "When I go preaching the Gospel of the kingdom, which means that Jesus defeated the devil and paid my debt of sin in full, it's time for a change. When I preach that I have the anointing to help change come about, the Lord will work with me and confirm the Word with signs following."

John Alexander Dowie had that "air" about him. His appearance inspired confidence, for he was full of authority. In his great crusade against unrighteousness, Dowie established a standard. He could probably be considered an apostle and a prophet in his own right.

He did not establish the standard of a denomination or a religious system; he established a standard by declaring God's will to heal the sick. When he came on the scene, the majority of people in the world were completely ignorant of the message of divine healing.

Through his large church and crusades, his Healing Homes, and the publicity he attracted, millions around the world came to know that God still heals today.

On New Year's Day 1900, Dowie unveiled plans for his dream city of Zion, which was built 40 miles north of Chicago as a wholesome environment for his followers and their families.

Recipe for Miracles

In order to have the miracles Dowie experienced in Chicago's climate of unbelief, and in order to believe that what you are believing is not off the deep end, you must make the following decision daily: "I believe the Word of God; therefore, I do not need the approval of the majority."

There are Christians in the Church today who cannot commit to the Great Commission because they have never seen it in action! They won't lay hands on the sick, and they won't see miracles, because persecution is associated with a flourishing Gospel, and they fear controversy, failure, and being persecuted. You don't get persecuted much when you're not flourishing. You don't get persecuted much when you're preaching something that is poverty-stricken, sin-infested, and disease-ridden. But the moment you believe in and stand for a life-changing Gospel, there's persecution!

John Alexander Dowie was persecuted. The religious system said, "We don't want him. He stirs up too much trouble."

Can you imagine a man who singlehandedly built Holy Ghost Healing Homes as an alternative to hospitals? After the world had given up on them, the sick came, heard the Word, were prayed for, and usually left totally healed.

So many people were healed, Dowie's healing ministry affected the medical community financially, and doctors opposed him. There was no love lost between them. Dowie hated medicine. He hated crutches. He hated disease.

An Imprint on Society

I don't want you to read this and say, "Christian Harfouche hates medicine and doctors." But I want you to know that a man like Dowie can come from a background of religiosity and get a revelation in the Word that becomes so powerful in him that he leaves his imprint on society a hundred years later. That is awesome!

I believe Dowie was a forerunner of the Healing Movement. As a matter of fact, when Dowie began to preach healing, few others were preaching it. He and Maria Woodworth-Etter were among the first.

Lay hands on yourself and say, "I not only have the Word; I also have the Spirit. I will flow with the power of both to see greater results, if I only believe and contend for the faith that was delivered to me."

Chapter 3
Living in the Realm of Miracles

A nd as Jesus passed by, he saw a man which was blind
from his birth.

And his disciples asked him, saying, Master, who did sin,
this man, or his parents, that he was born blind?

Jesus answered, Neither hath this man sinned, nor his
parents: but that the works of God should be made manifest in him.

I must work the works of him that sent me, while it is
day: the night cometh, when no man can work.

As long as I am in the world, I am the light of the world.

John 9:1-5

Jesus passed by with His 12 disciples. They were right
next to a man who was born blind when the disciples asked
Jesus, "Rabbi, who sinned — this man or his parents — that
he was born blind?"

That was the common theology of the day. It seems like
that theology is still in business today, because when we see
someone who is suffering from a seemingly hopeless condition, we try to find a *reason* for why they are like that.

I want to challenge you. If you want to live successfully
in the realm of miracles, one principle you must remember is:
Do not try to find out why certain things are the way they are.
The moment you do, you will start conjuring up super-spiritual answers.

People frequently build a theology on why people don't
get healed. In other words, if you bring 10 blind people to a

service and only three get healed, people tend to build a theology on why the seven didn't get healed.

What you should say is, "Thank God, we got three healed! Let's have another service and bring the seven back. We'll get another three healed. Then there will only be four left. We'll have several more services, and we'll get them *all* healed."

Be careful not to analyze and try to formulate a doctrine about the cause of an impossibility. When the disciples asked Jesus who had sinned in the blind man's case, they were only repeating the theology that was predominant in their day.

All his life — anytime he was in the synagogue, anytime he heard a sermon preached, anytime he heard someone's opinion, anytime another rabbi passed by, anytime someone gave him alms — that blind man had heard this question.

Sin Before Birth?

Let's examine this attitude. First, how could you sin before birth and be born blind, unless you sinned in another life, which we know does not happen.

But the Hindus, who believe in reincarnation, would look at someone who is blind, crippled, or otherwise handicapped, and say, "The reason they're like that is because it's *karma*." In other words, what they did in a former life caused providence to allow this to come on them.

If we're not careful, we'll be Christians in church and Buddhists or Hindus in lifestyle, because we think, "Well, the reason the Lord is allowing that person to be sick is because someone sinned."

What's the Reason?

When Paul survived a shipwreck and reached the island of Malta, the natives exclaimed when the snake bit him, "Oh, he must be a murderer, because he didn't die in the sea and now the snake bit him. There's a reason for this!" Mankind is always trying to find a reason why there's an impossibility.

Do you realize *it's not what happens to you that matters; it's what you do with what happens to you.* Paul shook the snake back in the fire, and when the people saw he wasn't going to die, they were ready to believe what he had to say.

People must see your consistency "in season and out of season." Paul refused to believe God was allowing the snake to bite him in order to teach him something. He shook it right back into the fire, unwilling to die yet. That's divine authority!

Anytime you say, "Well, the reason it's not happening is because...," you're being super-spiritual, because Jesus Christ is the same yesterday, today, and forever! If He's not being the same today in your life, it's because you might not be meeting the challenge God has called you to walk in.

The Normal Helpless Condition

The disciples were displaying the normal helpless condition of mortals. In other words, we can't do anything about a man born blind, so there must be a *reason* for it.

"So tell us, Master, who did sin — this man; *karma*, that he was born blind; or his parents? It must be generational." Yes, there is a truth to generational problems or weaknesses, but those conditions can be broken by believing prayer.

The last time I went to the doctor for a checkup, even though nothing was wrong with me, I was given a long list to fill out. It asked, Does this run in your family? Does that run in your family?

The doctor looks at that list when you see him. Then he says, "Based on the fact that such-and-such disease runs in your family, you ought to be having regular checkups to make sure you don't have it, because chances are you're going to get it."

The Preacher Answers

When the doctor looked at my questionnaire, all my answers were no, no, no, no, no. *Nothing* is running in this family but divine health, glory to God, because we broke everything bad that was handed down. We're not going to let it run in this family any longer, because there shall no plague come nigh the dwelling of this family. We don't let it!

The doctor looked at my questionnaire and said, "You're a preacher, huh?" I did not have to preach a sermon to him; he knew what I believed from reading my chart.

Normal, helpless, powerless humans say, "There must be a *reason* for this!" If you allow yourself to be bound up in the realm of reason, you will never be moved by faith to act. But the moment you move to act, you will be given all the power you need to see change come about in your life.

The Work of God

This is what Jesus replied in John 9:3-5:

Neither hath this man sinned, nor his parents; but that the works of God should be made manifest in him.

I must work the works of him that sent me, while it is day: the night cometh, when no man can work.

As long as I am in the world, I am the light of the world.

Notice *it wasn't blindness that was the work of God; it was what Jesus was about to do that was the work of God* so the works of God would be made manifest. Jesus said, "Never mind the reason. Neither this man nor his parents have sinned."

Also notice that Jesus just said, "Unless I do the works of Him that sent Me, the works of God would not be manifested in people." He later gave His authority to the Church, and now *we* can say, "Unless we work, the works of God will not be manifested in people's lives."

So if we do not do the works of Him that sent us, we will not see the works of God manifested in people's lives. Jesus said, "As long as I am in the world, I must do. I am the light of the world. I must do."

What is blindness? It's a work of the devil. What is blindness? It's a by-product of the curse.

A Different Sermon

The blind man was sitting right there, and he could hear what Jesus was saying. After all, he wasn't *deaf*; he was just blind.

For the first time in his life, he heard a *different* sermon. He heard a sermon that emphasized the reason why things were the way they were. All his life, he had believed his blindness was caused either by him or his parents. But this day he heard a sermon that said, "Never mind the reason. I can change things." The moment you give a sermon like that, people start listening.

There are people in the earth today who feel, like the blind man, that the reason they're going through things is because of God. Some people think that the reason they don't see miracles is because of God. Others think the reason they don't succeed is because of God.

The moment the blind man heard this different report, he started listening intently.

Jesus said, "I must work the works of him that sent me, while it is day: the night cometh, when no man can work. As long as I am in the world, I am the light of the world."

The Healing of the Blind Man

The story continues:

When he had thus spoken, he spat on the ground, and made clay of the spittal, and he anointed the eyes of the blind man with the clay.

And said unto him, Go, wash in the pool of Siloam, (which is by interpretation, Sent.) He went his way therefore, and washed, and came seeing.

John 9:6,7

When the blind man heard Jesus talking to the disciples, he thought, "You mean it's not my fault? You mean it's not my *karma*? You mean it's not my lot in life? You mean it's not my parents' fault? You mean God didn't put this on me?

"You mean the works of God should be made manifest in me? You mean blindness is not the work of God? He's the light of the world? I've never seen light. I need light. He must do the works of Him that sent Him? I wonder who sent Him? I wonder what His works are?"

Jesus Knows the Need

Then he heard Jesus spitting — and it wasn't a delicate, Charismatic spit, either, because you can't make clay that way. The significance is, Jesus hadn't even spoken to the blind man yet. Jesus hadn't asked him anything, but He was indirectly communicating with the man's spirit, because He knew the man's need.

The moment we begin to know what the need is, and that we have an answer to that need, people will listen, and they will have a miracle.

As Jesus was spitting, the blind man was thinking, "What is He doing?" Notice the word *"doing."* Jesus had said, "I must *do* the works." The blind man figured He was doing something good.

Jesus made the clay. He approached the blind man, and the blind man was ready, even though he hasn't been spoken to yet.

For the first time, he was exonerated. For the first time, he was justified. He wasn't told, "It's your fault." He wasn't told, "It's up to God." He was told, "I am here as a Messenger. I can do something." And he was willing to listen.

Then Jesus put the clay on his eyes, telling him, "Go, wash in the pool of Siloam." That's all He said. And the man went, and washed, and came back seeing. The only "work" Jesus did was to issue a command to the blind man.

A Thirst for Healing

That's why John Alexander Dowie insisted, "Stop taking the morphine, or I won't pray for you. Come back later, when you're in a lot of pain, and I'll pray for you then."

When you have a gift from God, you should not "cast your pearls before swine," or pour it out indiscriminately. First, you must develop the thirst for it in your own life and then you must develop the thirst for it in someone else's life to get them to receive.

Covered With Faith

Jesus never told the blind man, "You'll come back seeing." As a matter of fact, He never told him, "I'm going to open your eyes." And He never told the disciples, "I'm going to open his eyes." He just hinted at it. *But He covered that man with so much faith, the man was healed!*

A blind man is conspicuous enough without mud on his face, but he is much more of an attention-getter with mud on his face.

As he went his way, someone asked, "Where are you going, blind man?"

"Just direct me to the pool of Siloam, the pool called Sent."

"Why are you going there?"

"Someone sent me there."

"Who sent you there?"

"Someone that was sent by Someone else."

"Well, what was He sent to do?"

"He was sent to do the works of Him who sent Him. He said He was the light of the world."

"Why do you have mud on your eyes?"

"Someone put mud on my eyes."

"Who?"

"Someone that was sent by Someone else."

"What was He sent to do?"

"He was sent to do the works of HIm that sent Him."

"Well, what did He do?"

"He put mud on my eyes, and He sent me."

"Where did He send you?"

"To the pool called Sent."

"Why are you going there?"

"I'm going there to wash the mud off my eyes."

A Walk of Faith

All the way to the pool, Jesus had this blind man in faith; he couldn't think about anything else. As he was walking down the road, the sun beat on the mud, and the mud dried up. The blind man was very conscious of the mud on his eyes.

He thought, "There's mud on my eyes. Who put mud on my eyes? The man who was sent by Someone else. What did He do? He sent me. Where did He send me? To the pool called Sent. What did He send me to do? To wash. What did He say? He said it wasn't my fault, and it wasn't my parents' fault!"

All the way to the pool, the blind man was not thinking about what the doctor said. He didn't care what his relatives said. He didn't care what the Pharisees said. He didn't care what public opinion said. He was so wrapped up in this rabbi's illustrated sermon that even though Jesus never said, "You will come back seeing," the blind man figured it out on his way to the pool.

"Light of the world? Doing the works of Him that sent Him? Spit? Mud on the eyes? Born blind — why? Never mind. I think that when I wash, I am going to receive my sight!"

Probably a crowd had gathered around him and was following him. He got to the pool and washed. Just like that, he received his sight!

Who Is the Light of the World?

Who is the light of the world? True, in John 9:5 Jesus said, "As long as I am in the world, I am the light of the world." But in Matthew 5:14-16, He said:

Ye are the light of the world. A city that is set on an hill cannot be hid.

Neither do men light a candle, and put it under a bushel, but on a candlestick; and it giveth light unto all that are in the house.

Let your light so shine before men, that they may see your good works, and glorify your Father which is in heaven.

Notice when Jesus said, "I am the light of the world," He was talking about doing a miracle; about doing the works of God. Then He said that *we* are the light of the world, and we are to let our light shine.

The Will of God Prevails

How does our light shine? *When we do the works of Him that sent us!* Then His will and His works are manifested in the lives of others. Where there used to be deafness as the will of Satan, now there is hearing. It is the will of God. Where there used to be blindness as the will of Satan, now there is sight. It is the will of God.

So Jesus said, "Let your light so shine before men, that they may see your good works." These good works are the result of His power. They are done by us to give Him glory.

When Jesus said, "I must do," He wasn't doing the miracle as God; He was doing the miracle as a man anointed by the Holy Spirit. The man Christ Jesus was saying, "In order for the will and the work of God to be done in that man, I must do it." The man Christ Jesus was saying, "I must work in order for people to see the power of God."

We in the Church today must realize that we were also sent. How were we sent? Jesus said, "As my Father hath sent me, even so send I you" (John 20:21).

If we know we were sent, what were we sent to do?

The works of Him that sent us.

Who sent us?

Jesus.

Who sent Him?
The Father.
What were we called to do?
The works of God — and we are going to do them!

Chapter 4
Living in the Anointing

And the apostles said unto the Lord, Increase our faith.

And the Lord said, If ye had faith as a grain of mustard seed, ye might say unto this sycamine tree, Be thou plucked up by the root, and be thou planted in the sea, and it should obey you.

Luke 17:5,6

When the disciples asked Jesus for faith, Jesus told them about the action-kind of faith — faith you can see. You can't see faith, but you can definitely see the *results* of active faith.

When a person is living by action faith, miracles, signs, and the witness of the Holy Spirit accompany his life, and he is successful.

So Jesus responded in verse 6, "If ye had faith as a grain of mustard seed, ye might say unto this sycamine tree, Be thou plucked up by the root, and be thou planted in the sea, and it should obey you."

That tells me that faith can produce a statement of command that is obeyed by an impossible condition.

As you know, in the natural a tree will not obey you. When Jesus said to the fig tree, "Let no fruit grow on thee henceforth for ever" (Matthew 21:19), it was a statement of faith that released the power of God, went right into the roots of that tree, and caused it to wither.

When the disciples saw it, they exclaimed, "Look how quickly the tree you commanded to wither has dried up!"

Jesus replied in Matthew 21:21,22:

If ye have faith, and doubt not, ye shall not only do this which is done to the fig tree, but also if ye shall say unto this mountain, Be thou removed, and be thou cast into the sea; it shall be done.

And all things, whatsoever ye shall ask in prayer, believing, ye shall receive.

My Words Can Carry a Miracle!

This tells me that active faith will produce a response. And it tells me *my words can carry a miracle* if they are words I believe are in line with God's Word; words I believe cannot fail.

There is something awesome about God's ability to impart faith that will, in turn, move you to speak to your situation and will bring a miracle.

However, there are certain signs and wonders that will never happen unless you do the commanding. One of them is *demonic situations.* God is not going to bind the devil for you, and He's not going to cast him out for you! If the devil is going to be cast out, it must be by your word. And he *will* obey your word!

Jesus said, "If I with the finger of God cast out devils, no doubt the kingdom of God is come upon you" (Luke 11:20). That phrase "the finger of God" means the power of God. Therefore, if Jesus cast out devils with His Word, His Word had power. The power was in the Word, and it literally drove the devil out, because it brought the power of God on the scene.

"What a Word Is This!"

And [he] came down to Capernaum, a city of Galilee, and taught them on the sabbath days.

And they were astonished at his doctrine: for his word was with power.

> And in the synagogue there was a man, which had a spirit of an unclean devil, and cried out with a loud voice,
>
> Saying, Let us alone; what have we to do with thee, thou Jesus of Nazareth? art thou come to destroy us? I know thee who thou art; the Holy One of God.
>
> And Jesus rebuked him, saying, Hold thy peace, and come out of him...
>
> Luke 4:31-35

In other words, Jesus said, "Shut up, and come out of him!"

> And when the devil had thrown him in the midst, he came out of him, and hurt him not.
>
> And they were all amazed, and spake among themselves, saying, What a word is this! for with authority and power he commandeth the unclean spirits, and they come out.
>
> Luke 4:35,36

Notice, Jesus was in the synagogue teaching, and while He was teaching, a man with an unclean devil started crying out. Anytime you flow in the anointing, it will cause the devil to react. Anytime you speak and live in the anointing, you will clash with the devil.

People who are demonized will "twitch" around you! They will shake around you. Sometimes they will become angry and cuss around you, because when you flow in the anointing, it causes the devil to manifest. It drives him to surface.

Why? Because the devil is in the business of hiding. He is not running around planet Earth saying, "I am real"; he is doing his best to make people believe that he really doesn't exist! He delights in working in secret. He likes darkness. He likes being camouflaged and going incognito.

The Spotlight of God Reveals Evil

But when you come on the scene with the Word and the anointing, the spotlight of God zeroes right in on the devil and makes him feel as if he's naked or uncovered.

That's why, when we testify, witness, or preach in the anointing, we are not shooting into the air or fighting the air. We are zeroing in and hitting spiritual powers head on, just like Jesus did when he dealt with the woman at the well of Samaria.

He hit the problems in that woman's life head on, and immediately brought to light the fact that His knowledge came by supernatural means.

When we testify, witness, or preach in the anointing, it will cause a response: People will be pricked in their hearts. They will either be converted, or they will rebel. They will either want to receive what we have, or they will become angry and want to stop us.

I was in a certain meeting recently, and I had a word of knowledge about multiple herniated discs in the back. I stepped in front of the pulpit ready to give it when I sensed a man was standing to my right. I turned and asked him, "What do you need, sir?" He said, "I have two herniated discs in my back."

I said, "You should have waited. I was getting ready to call that out."

He said, "Well, I'm here now."

Resisting the Power of God

As I laid hands on him and began to minister to him, I felt the virtue of God flowing through me, yet there was something that rose up from within him — an attitude, a disposition, a critical attitude, unbelief — that resisted the power of God, and it bounced off him. I knew he wasn't receiving, so I removed my hands. He began to walk off the platform in a huff, with an attitude.

I said, "Sir, come back here! Come here. Do you believe God sent me here to heal you?"

And this is what he said: "I believe that He *can*, if He wants to."

That was a rebellious attitude he had, in light of the fact that I had just finished preaching from the Word of God for an hour on God's willingness to bless people with their miracle!

While I was preaching, evidently this man was flipping through his Bible trying to find something that contradicted what I was saying. And because of this, I knew he was not going to receive his miracle.

Righteous Indignation

I felt righteous indignation rise up on the inside of me. The Lord had shown me there were other people in that building with the same condition he had. I said to him, "Sir, just stand there and watch." Then I announced, "If you are here tonight, and you have a multiple herniated condition in your back, I want you to come up here right now. I'm going to minister to you, and God is going to heal you."

The first man who came up was in excruciating pain. I asked him, "Do you believe God sent me here to heal you?" He replied, "I *know* God sent you here to heal me!" When I laid my hands on him, he fell under the power. He was instantly healed by the power of God.

I asked the same question of the next man who came up. I said, "Do you believe God sent me here to heal you?" "Yes," he said. Immediately I laid hands on him. He started jumping up and down, shouting and praising God.

I said to the man who doubted, "Just watch. This is how easy it is. Just look."

The third man who came had not turned his head for nine years because his neck was stiff. I put my hands on his neck. I asked, "Do you believe God sent me here to heal you?" He said, "Yes."

I said, "Well, then, you shouldn't have that stiff neck, should you?" I turned his neck, and it turned easily in every direction. He was instantly healed by the power of the living God.

Clash With the Devil!

In order to flow in that realm of miracles, you must clash with the devil — and you *will* clash with the devil. However, you won't clash with the devil if you pray nice little prayers and don't pursue him beyond that point.

A man whose bones had been eaten up with disease for 20 years came to one of our meetings. He was in excruciating pain. His face told the story.

He had pain in his chest, pain in his vertebrae, pain in his joints, and so forth. He had to use a walking stick to get around.

Before I laid my hands on him, I asked him, "Do you believe God sent me here to heal you?"

He shook his head and said, "I *want* to believe." When I laid my hands on him, he fell under the power. His expression mirrored his thoughts: "I'm not healed. I'm not going to get healed. I'm in pain. I shouldn't be lying on the floor."

Why? Because he had a disease, it was eating his bones, and he was in agony.

That man would never have received his miracle unless I stood him up, grabbed him by the hands, and told him, "Open your eyes and look at me!" In the spirit I detected in him self-pity, a spirit of hopelessness, and a will to lie down and let the devil have his way in his life.

A Time for Decision

I said, "I'm not going to allow you to leave here without your miracle! You can either make the choice to lie down and let the devil cripple you, or you can make the decision to stand up and receive your miracle!"

Then I told him, "The doctors can't help you anymore — but Jesus can!"

I picked up his hands and lifted them above his head, something he hadn't been able to do. I took away his walking stick, but he didn't need it any longer. His pain was gone!

His response was, "I can't believe it! I don't have any pain! I can't believe it!"

I said, *"Believe* it!"

We're not going to see miracles unless we clash with the devil. We can't have miracles by praying little prayers and allowing the devil to hide in people's lives, even if he's hiding in the form of a misconception or an attitude of pity or hopelessness. You have to confront it. You have to drive it to the surface and take command of the situation. But first you must believe in what you know, and you must know what God said.

When Excuses Are Demolished

We have been studying the story of Jesus teaching in the synagogue of Nazareth. The devil couldn't handle his teaching anointing.

I've been in meetings where people crossed their legs so many times, they wore out their pants! They were uncomfortable because the truth was being preached. They were "itchy," looking at everything they could look at because the devils that were binding them with tradition were being knocked down, one after another, and they couldn't handle the fact that their excuses were being demolished right in front of their eyes. It was a time of deliverance.

As Jesus was teaching, a man suddenly cried out with a loud voice. It was a full demonic manifestation. What are the odds that the same demon-possessed man was in the synagogue every Sabbath for years, and no one knew he had a devil until Jesus showed up? It's entirely possible, because the devil can hide quite well when there is no anointing. But the moment the anointing is flowing, you will see demonic manifestations. They will come to the surface.

How To Talk to Devils

You and I have been called by God to do two things: heal the sick and cast out devils. This means we have to know how to talk to devils and cast them out. There is an attitude involved in talking to the devil, and there is a power involved in releasing those words.

The devils in the demon-possessed man spoke to Jesus and said, "What have we to do with You? Have You come to destroy us?" Jesus made His reply short and plain: "Shut up, and come out!" Isn't that plain?

As I was preaching in a meeting in Florida, the people had jumped to their feet and I was pacing up and down the aisle. A man standing in the front held his hands together and said in a deep, guttural voice, "Come here."

I went over to him, grabbed his hands, and said to the devils in him, "Shut up, in Jesus' Name!" He fell to his knees. I said, "Say 'Jesus.'" He said, "Jesus." "Say, 'Thank You for setting me free right now.'" He was instantly delivered, and we went on with the service.

Most of the time, if the devil cannot hide, he will do his best to get as much attention as he can. If he has to manifest, he wants it to be so flashy and strong that you are captivated or moved by fear rather than by the Word of God.

So Jesus told the devil to shut up, and He cast him out. Luke 4:36 says, "They were all amazed, and spake among themselves, saying, What a word is this! for with authority and power he commandeth the unclean spirits, and they come out."

Chapter 5
Day of Impartation

Now I want to share with you about another "child of destiny," John G. Lake, the great missionary to Africa who was used powerfully in the area of deliverance.

Lake was the kind of man who believed it was God's will to redeem spirit, soul, and body, so he believed that every part of man can be charged with the life of God. He was not planning to get sick or fail, because he believed that God's anointing and redemptive plan included every part of his being.

Lake is well known for the fact that during the time the bubonic plague hit South Africa, he conducted an experiment, putting his hand in froth that was infected with the virus. Under the scrutiny of a microscope, the scientific community watched while the disease died because it was touched by the man of God!

But it wasn't always like that for John G. Lake. He and his relatives were often sick. Sickness and disease, doctors and nurses, hospitals, funerals, graveyards, and tombstones were memories that haunted his early childhood and young life like a nightmare. I believe Lake developed an unnatural hatred for sickness and disease because of these early experiences.

When you realize it is not God's will to kill, steal, and destroy, and when you realize that you have been given the power to do something about it, you begin to hate it, and you begin to do what you can to annihilate its influence on the lives of people.

"I Walked Like a Christian"

For a long time, John G. Lake suffered from rheumatism. His legs were crooked. His pastor told him he was glorifying God by his rheumatism. And his church told him to endure it.

But he went to John Alexander Dowie's Healing Home at 12th and Michigan Streets in Chicago, where an old gray-haired man laid hands on Lake. The power of God went through him and made his legs straight. "I went out and walked on the street like a Christian," Lake recalled.

A Christian ought to have straight legs, a straight back, and a straight walk. That's what Lake believed — that redemption wasn't meant only to save our soul; it can also renew our mind, heal our body, and fill us with the life and energy of God. That was the key to Lake's boldness to dare to put his hands in the plague-infected froth.

Someone may say, "Well, I might try that some day." Don't do it! It's not something we *try*. Lake did it because he knew that he knew that he knew that he wasn't on planet Earth to catch a disease; he was here to deal with the disease through the power of the living God.

Transmission and Impartation

When he went to John Alexander Dowie's Healing Home, Lake experienced a miracle. I'm sharing this with you to show you there is a transmission and impartation that passes from one ministry to another. It enables the newer ministry to carry a torch that is similar to and sometimes greater than the torch that the established ministry carried.

Today is a day of impartation. We are going to do the same thing. Such as we have, we are going to give unto you, because there is a torch, an impartation, that gives you a supernatural ability to contend for the great things in God.

Lake became a successful businessman. He made a lot of money in business and later worked in Dowie's ministry. During his time of training as a faithful man, Lake got a bit critical and criticized Dowie.

Dowie confronted him and told him, "If you ever develop constructive qualities equal to your critical capacity, you will be a bigger man than I am. At present, however, you are an operator, not a constructor. But you have it in you."

Sometimes you have to be stirred like this. I don't believe Lake would ever have become what God wanted him to be if he hadn't experienced the confronting reality of the man of God.

Lake got delivered from his criticism, and instead of leaving Dowie's ministry critical and broken, he left with the same torch and the same miracle-level anointing he saw operating in Dowie's life.

Also, because Dowie challenged him, and because Lake was a teachable man, we find that Lake later went to South Africa and built a work that comprised 700,000 members.

A Form of Deliverance

Records tell us that one day as Lake was ministering, a group of ruffians entered the church and started toward the platform. Lake immediately perceived that the young men were up to no good. With him on the platform were a band and a choir made up of women and girls.

While the ushers were still scrambling to come to his aid, Lake quickly solved the problem. As the ruffians came on the platform, he grabbed them by the seat of the pants and the back of the neck and literally threw them out the window that was located above his head.

One...two...three...and the rest noticed that this man must be operating in supernatural strength. They decided not to come up on the platform. The same Holy Spirit who came upon Samson came upon John G. Lake that day.

Lake believed not only in a Holy Spirit who blesses your heart; he believed in a Holy Spirit who influences your body. That's why he wouldn't catch a germ or a disease. That's why he had supernatural strength when the situation demanded it.

I know some well-meaning Christians will say, "That's cruel, isn't it, to throw people out of a window?" If you look at it one way, it's cruel. But in another way, Lake might have had an altar call that night and filled the altar with people who respected the man of God who had such strength.

We have to know what we know, we have to believe what we know, and we have to believe what God said. John G. Lake was like that.

The Dangers of Religious "Salad"

Lake was in a certain meeting in South Africa when a woman with a crutch came up to the platform and asked for prayer. She had spent a great deal of money seeing doctors. Nothing had helped her, and now she was seeing what they called hypnotists. (Today they may call them psychologists, because hypnotism is often part of their treatment.)

Lake asked, "Where's your hypnotist now?" She said, "He's sitting in the front."

Lake simply stepped out and said, "You devil of hypnotism, come out of him!" He didn't even know who the man was. He added, "And enter into him no more." Then he went on ministering to the woman, who was instantly healed.

After that meeting was over, the hypnotist came to Lake and offered him a large sum of money to give him back the ability to hypnotize people, because it left him upon Lake's prayer.

Today some people want psychology, psychiatry, hypnotism, Christian Science, New Age, and everything else that seems right. They want to mix it together in a "salad" of religious persuasion and come out with the kind of results Dowie and Lake had. But you can't do it that way. You must learn to discern who the devil is; you must learn to discern what is of the devil; and you've got to know how to confront it.

Breaking Up a Seance

At times Lake would go to a seance, just to break it up! He liked to confront the spiritualists and bind any demons that might be present. Once he went to a seance that was attended by a husband and wife, Methodists, who had lost their born-again daughter.

The spiritualist medium was supposedly conjuring up the "spirit" of this dead girl and communicating with her.

After the girl's so-called "spirit" spoke, Lake said, "Let me talk to her spirit now," and the medium let him.

He asked the spirit, "Are you So-and-so?" A female voice answered, "Yes, I am."

"Where were you born?" The voice gave him the right information.

"Where did you grow up?" Again the voice gave him the correct answer.

"Then you were there in the church that night when I gave the altar call, and you came forward to the altar and gave your life to the Lord."

The spirit couldn't remember that. Do you know why? Because the moment the spirit remembered it, Lake would ask the next question: "So you believe that Jesus Christ is come in the flesh, don't you?" And the spirit would have to answer in the affirmative.

"You mean you don't remember the time when you were baptized in the Holy Ghost?"

"No, I don't remember that."

"Then you're not that girl, you lying devil! Get out of here now" — and the spirit left!

We need more men and women of God who can crash a seance or a psychic rally. We need believers who know how to operate in the anointing of God. John Lake knew how to live in that realm and dimension where the power of God operated strongly through him.

100,000 Documented Healings

Lake said, "Throw your medicine in the toilet and then apologize to the toilet." I'm just quoting him. Today I know he might seem extreme, but he had extreme results, too: 100,000 documented miracles of healing in the city of Spokane, Washington, where he established Healing Rooms and healing services. Those are extreme results!

A man like John G. Lake is entitled to his opinions. He was a man of absolutes. When he believed something, he stuck to it. There's something admirable about that. I believe there's a place in God like that, and I believe Jesus walked there.

I don't believe that Jesus walked around with a medicine cabinet carried by the disciples so he could take some medicine when He broke down between meetings. No! I believe Jesus was walking in that level where He did not need medicine. He *was* the medicine! He was the Balm of Gilead. He was the Great Physician.

Walking in Perfect Health

Potentially, we also have divine health, and we can walk in it. Lake did. He walked in perfect health when it came to his physical state.

I believe a certain amount of Lake's antagonism toward medicine and his refusal to tolerate any alternative to divine healing came about because he was so well acquainted with John Alexander Dowie's ministry, and he saw so many results there — more results than you would normally see in a hospital or a doctor's office.

Lake therefore formed his theology on what the Bible says about divine healing, and it's strong. That's why he could crash a seance, or tell you to throw away your medicine.

Lake worked hard. He preached six times a week and twice on Sundays, but he never burned out — and he never fell out. He was consistent in his strength, because he believed that God lived on the inside of him.

You ask, "How will that help me live today?"

By finding out what these "children of destiny" thought, we can become what they were. If, by thinking the Word, they became the product of the Word, we can think the same way. As a man thinketh in his heart, so is he. The battle is in the mind. The moment we've conquered the mental battle, we will understand our spiritual authority.

Pentecost As God Gave It

A key to John G. Lake's ministry was a vision he had. An angel appeared to him, took him through the Book of Acts, and spoke these words to him: "This is Pentecost as God gave it." Among other things, he also said, "Strive for this. Contend for this. Teach the people to pray for this."

The angel took him through the miracles, the acts of the apostles, the moves of the Holy Spirit, and the results the Church enjoyed, including the salvation of the thousands. And he said, "This is Pentecost as God gave it."

In other words, "Anything else, John Lake — anything watered down, anything that is not as strong, anything that is not as radical — is not pure. *This is Pentecost as God gave it!*"

That vision, that revelation, produced the kind of man John G. Lake became: a bold man, a man of the Spirit and a man of the Word. We need both, and we're going to find out what God is saying about that shortly.

Occultic Resistance

And when they had gone through the isle unto Paphos, they found a certain sorcerer, a false prophet, a Jew, whose name was Bar-jesus.

Acts 13:6

Notice this man wasn't a Christian; he was a sorcerer. The Bible calls him a false prophet. It seems to me that much of what the Bible says about false prophets is referring to today's New Agers, occultists, and Satanists who deny the Lordship of Jesus Christ.

I believe with all of my heart that everyone in the Church of Jesus Christ has been included in the privilege of speaking on God's behalf. All of you at some time or other are going to speak on behalf of God in order to reach someone. And whenever you do that, you're God's messenger for that hour.

So whether we're called to the office of the prophet or we're a lay person, each of us is going to weave into a certain level of speaking God's Word into the lives of others.

Paul and Barnabas next met a government official:

...the deputy of the country, Sergius Paulus, a prudent man; who called for Barnabas and Saul, and desired to hear the word of God.

But Elymas the sorcerer (for so is his name by interpretation) withstood them, seeking to turn away the deputy from the faith.

Acts 13:7,8

Notice there is occultic resistance here to the miracle of salvation. In other words, whatever you set your hands to do, you are going to have to commit to it through obstances and resistance. There will be either natural or demonic reasons for why you should not succeed in doing what God has called you to do. That's why it is imperative to know who you are and to stick to the power God has given you.

Paul reacted strongly to the sorcerer's attempts to hinder the Gospel:

Then Saul, (who also is called Paul,) filled with the Holy Ghost, set his eyes on him,

And said, O full of all subtilty and all mischief, thou child of the devil, thou enemy of all righteousness, wilt thou not cease to pervert the right ways of the Lord?

And now, behold, the hand of the Lord is upon thee, and thou shalt be blind, not seeing the sun for a season. And immediately there fell on him a mist and a darkness; and he went about seeking some to lead him by the hand.

Then the deputy, when he saw what was done, believed, being astonished at the doctrine of the Lord.

Acts 13:9-12

The Bible says the deputy was astonished at the teaching. It was an illustrated sermon!

Chapter 6
Growing in the Anointing

We know that before Paul was released to his apostolic function as a "sent one," he was named among the prophets and the teachers that were in the church of Antioch. The Bible says so, and calls him by name:

> Now there were in the church that was at Antioch certain prophets and teachers, as Barnabas, and Simeon that was called Niger, and Lucius of Cyrene, and Manaen, which had been brought up with Herod the tetrarch, and Saul.
>
> As they ministered to the Lord, and fasted, the Holy Ghost said, Separate me Barnabas and Saul for the work whereunto I have called them.
>
> And when they had fasted and prayed, and laid their hands on them, they sent them away.
>
> Acts 13:1-3

We know that Paul was a man of visions and revelations. He wrote, "...I will come to visions and revelations of the Lord" (2 Corinthians 12:1).

So before Paul was sent out to function as an *apostle*, he was not only a *teacher* of the Gentiles; he was also a *prophet*. As a prophet of Jesus Christ, he had a certain level, capacity, function, and authority that accompanied him and enabled him to present Jesus on a high caliber of flow.

The Holy Spirit said, "Separate me Barnabas and Saul for the work whereunto I have called them" (Acts 13:2). And they laid hands on them, prayed over them, and released them to their ministries.

What did that accomplish? It was the impartation that brought the final level of anointing necessary to go out and fulfill their ministry. It was like an ordination or sealing to release the gifts of God in the two men in the level they needed.

So they departed on their mission to spread the Gospel, and the first thing they encountered was the challenge of a false prophet — head on. They were trying to convert a prominent, prudent man, but Elymas the sorcerer "withstood them."

The Bible doesn't say just *how* he withstood them. It doesn't say if he tried to put a curse on Paul and Barnabas. It doesn't say if he tried to bind the gift of Paul.

Cursing Weak Christians

Today there are Satanists who think they have more power than the Church does, and some of them are messing around and putting curses on weak Christians. And because these Christians receive the symptoms of headaches and confusion instead of rebuking them, they keep preying on them.

Sometimes Satanists or occultists will come into a meeting to try to hinder it. When we were in a recent meeting, a woman who was into spiritualism was present. Robin had a word of knowledge and called out, "Someone here is using beads and doing occultic things, and we want you to come up here for deliverance."

When the woman didn't come, I pointed her out to the whole church. The next week she attended another of my meetings and came up in the altar call because she wanted hands laid on her. She wanted to receive *the blessing,* she said, but she didn't want to receive Jesus Christ.

You see, people in the occult know there is power. Many of them are striving to have greater power, and some of them will try to oppose what you're doing.

The Roots of Epic Revival

When John Lake went to South Africa, his workers came back reporting that the witch doctors were resisting them. Lake got the people together and said, "I want you to go out into the mission field and find the witch doctors. I want you to openly challenge them, and I want you to cast the devil out of them."

When they did, and the people saw that greater is He that is in the Church than he that is in the witch doctors, people got saved and delivered, and revival broke out.

It is no different here in America. When the world finally sees that the occultists, the New Agers, the psychics, the spiritualists, and the Satanists do not pack more power than the Bible-believing children of the living God, we're going to see revival. And we're going to see it in epic proportions, because God has called you and me to confront the devil!

Mixing the Spirit and the Word

Immediately Paul did something: He told the devil off — in the Holy Ghost. You don't lack words when you're anointed. Too many people stop to think, "What am I going to say?" That isn't necessary when you mix the Spirit and the Word together in your daily life.

The apostles did this. They said, "We will give ourselves continually to prayer, and to the ministry of the Word" (Acts 6:4). What does that mean?

"We will get information and revelation from the Word. We will make it our foundation. Then, when we pray in tongues, it will build us up. We will get faith out of the Word, and we will be built up on that faith by praying in the Holy Ghost. And when we run into a situation that demands a miracle, we can deal with it."

Faith for Blindness

Paul dealt with the sorcerer by rebuking him and then telling him, "And now, behold, the hand of the Lord is upon thee, and thou shalt be blind, not seeing the sun for a season. And immediately there fell on him a mist and a darkness; and he went about seeking some to lead him by the hand" (Acts 13:11).

Paul had no problem with blindness. In fact, he had faith for blindness because of his own experience. When Paul (then Saul) was still a child of the devil by nature, he was persecuting and threatening the Church, even killing Christians, with the permission of the religious leaders.

Saul was on his way to persecute the church in Damascus when a light brighter than the noonday sun suddenly knocked him to the ground and blinded him.

The Bible says Saul heard a voice. It was Jesus asking him, "Saul, Saul, why persecutest thou me?" He replied, "Who art thou, Lord?" "I am Jesus whom thou persecutest..." (Acts 9:4,5).

Saul remained blind for three days until a believer in Damascus named Ananias prayed for him and he recovered his sight. That's why Paul had blind faith. He figured, "You mess with God, He'll strike you blind." It had happened to him.

A Sorcerer Goes Blind

Therefore, when he ran across his first sorcerer, Paul said, "I know how to deal with him. BAM — the hand of the Lord is on you!" And immediately the sorcerer went blind.

The Bible says when the deputy *saw* that doctrine, he quickly learned the lesson and believed. What was the doctrine? You mess with God, you get judgment. What was the doctrine? The power of God is greater than anything. What was the doctrine? There is active power in this message.

Peter, on the other hand, didn't have blind faith. Even though he was one of the disciples, he had denied the Lord three times shortly before His crucifixion. He was worthy to be a castaway, and he knew it.

After the resurrection, the Lord appeared to him in the Galilee and asked him three questions: "Do you love Me? Do you love Me? Do you love Me?" — and He restored Peter.

Peter knew one thing: You betray the Lord; you die. How did he know that? Judas had betrayed the Lord, and he had experienced suicide, death, and judgment. That was what Peter knew.

Later, when he was a leader in the Church, Peter ran into Ananias and Sapphira, who lied to the Holy Spirit. He knew what to do about their situation. What happens to you when you lie to the Holy Spirit? You die, that's what happens to you!

Peter asked Ananias and Sapphira, "Why did Satan fill your heart to lie to the Holy Ghost?" POW! — they dropped dead at his feet. The faith Peter had was killing faith. Paul's was blinding-for-a-few-days faith.

Growing Means Excelling

What am I expressing here? As you grow in your experience in God — as you grow in the anointing — you will excel in certain areas. Different persons in Church history have excelled at different things.

Even the healing ministries didn't have the same rate of success with every kind of disease. Some healing evangelists had the gift of healing for blindness, and they had more blind healed than any other condition. Others prayed more successfully for people with crippling conditions, hearing problems, cancer, and so forth.

Each of us has the potential to be successful in every area, but there will usually be an area in which our faith flows the easiest. For example, some people can believe God for money. Some people can't. Some people can believe God for money, but they remain sick. Others stay poor but remain healthy.

God's best is for us to be able to believe for *everything* He has made available to us.

A Frozen Intruder

I was in Hollywood, California, ministering in a prayer line when a rugged, loud, unruly man came up to the altar and began to shout, trying to disrupt the service.

I went over there and asked, using the live microphone, "Do you need prayer?"

He said, "I'm here, aren't I?" I repeated the question. "I'm going to ask you one more time: 'Do you need prayer?'" "I'm here, aren't I?"

I said, "Either you say you need prayer, or you go over there right now and sit down and be quiet." He said, "Yeah, I need prayer."

I grabbed his hand and said, "I bind you, devil, in the Name of Jesus! You will *not* disrupt this service!" And I walked away. That man stood there *frozen* until I finished praying for everyone. When we dismissed the service, he left the building.

Acting Before You Think

You see, there will be certain times when a challenge will unexpectedly confront you, and you won't have time to think, "What would Jesus do in this situation?" or "What am I supposed to do?"

You needn't wonder, because when you're full of the Holy Spirit and the Word, you can act before you think. You can know that what you're going to say and do is going to be backed up by the power of God.

That is why and how Paul was able to speak out of the Spirit of God that was within him a word that brought conviction and reality into the lives of people.

Speaking to the Devil

In Matthew 8:16 it says, "When the even was come, they brought unto him many that were possessed with devils, and he cast out the spirits with his word, and healed all that were sick."

Jesus cast out the devils with His Word, and He healed all that were sick. Notice there is a way to flow. Once we understand what the root of a situation is, we can immediately know by the Spirit what to do.

We must speak by faith to the devil and tell him to go. We can bind him, and he will be bound. We can loose the power of God, and it will be loosed. When we operate in that realm, we will see great things!

Talking to Tumors

When I was in Hawaii, a man flew in from Canada. He had 40 tumors the size of golf balls hanging on the outside of his body. He had been prayed for by several "greats" in the healing ministry. He named them to me. It was almost as if he was trying to convince me that he had a track record in *not* being healed.

I told him, "I'm not going to pray for you then." His eyes got real big. "I'm not here to pray for you," I explained, "because I'm here to get you healed! I'm going to curse those tumors. I'm not going to pray that God would heal you. I'm going to talk to those tumors. I'm going to tell them to dissolve, and they're going to have to dissolve."

Within a few days, only four of the 40 tumors were left, and several days later, he didn't have any. He came up to the platform, removed his shirt to testify, and rejoiced at his healing.

Why was he healed? Because we *targeted* the problem. We spoke to it. We released that power resident in us through the Holy Spirit to go to work in that body and see it manifest the power and the anointing of the Lord.

Learning From the Greats

Men like Dowie and Lake had a mighty role to play in the church world. If we can glean from them some of the revelations they had and the truths they held dear, we can incorporate it into what we know to be the truth. If something is Bible-based, you can bank on it.

In closing this segment devoted to John G. Lake, I want to share the following prophetic word attributed to him. This man was so under the anointing of the Lord, he prophesied this utterance in perfect rhyme.

Prophecy Given by John G. Lake

He is risen! He is risen! Hear the cry
Ringing through the land and sea and sky.
'Tis the shout of victory: Triumph is proclaimed.
Heralds of God announce it: Death's disdained.

Shout the tidings! Shout the tidings! Raise the cry:
Christ's victorious, Christ's victorious, cannot die.
For the bars of death He sundered;
Satan sees that he has blundered.
As the shouts of angels thundered: "He's alive!"

Catch the shout, ye earth-born mortals. Let it roll
Till it echoes o'er the mountains, from the centre to the poles,
That the Christ of earth and Glory
Death has conquerered. Tell the story:
He's the victor, He's the victor! So am I.

For this reason, that my ransom He has paid,
I've accepted His atonement, on Him laid.
He the Lamb of God that suffered all for me,
Bore my sins, my grief, my sickness on the tree.

I am risen, I am risen, from the grave
Of my sins, my griefs, my sickness; and the waves
Of the resurrection life and holy power
Thrill my being with His new life every hour.

Now the lightnings of God's Spirit burn my soul;
Flames of His divine compassion o'er me roll.
Lightning power of God's own Spirit strikes the power of hell.
God in man — oh, glory, glory! — all the story tell.

I have proved Him, I have proved Him. It is true:
Christ's dominion yet remaineth; 'tis for you.
Let the fires of holy passion sweep your soul.
Let the Christ who death has conquered take control.
He will use you, He will use you, Zion yet has saviors still.
Christ the Conqueror only waiteth for the action of your will.

Lake prophesied this extemporaneously by the anointing of the Holy Spirit on June 18, 1910 in South Africa. It was supernatural, and it carried a revelation in it.

Lake prophesied, "My sickness was carried. My griefs were carried. My sins were carried on the tree. God was waiting for me just to make that my will."

Lake had more revelation of the cross of Calvary and the triumph of the resurrection than most of the Body of Christ and some theologians have today. Is it any wonder he couldn't catch the plague? Is it any wonder he could throw people out a high window?

Let us yield to the Holy Spirit, step out of natural limits, and speak, live, and act supernaturally!

Chapter 7
The Key to Miracles

In the eighth chapter of Acts we read that the apostles appointed deacons to wait on tables. The apostles said:

> ...It is not reason that we should leave the word of God, and serve tables.
>
> Wherefore, brethren, look ye out among you seven men of honest report, full of the Holy Ghost and wisdom, whom we may appoint over this business.
>
> But we will give ourselves continually to prayer, and to the ministry of the word.
>
> And the saying pleased the whole multitude: and they chose Stephen, a man full of faith and of the Holy Ghost....
>
> **Acts 6:2-5**

I want you to see something that I believe is the key to having miracles in your life. There are two elements you must have for miracles, and you cannot have one without the other: prayer and the Word.

Notice the apostles said they would give themselves continually "to prayer, and to the ministry of the word." That means, we need not only the teaching of the Word, but we also need prayer so we may be filled with the Holy Spirit.

One of the men they chose to wait on tables was Stephen, who later became the first martyr of the Church. The Bible says that he was a man full of faith and the Holy Spirit.

Elements for Ministry

Notice the two different elements in him: faith and the Holy Spirit. You can be full of faith and not be full of the Holy Spirit.

We have seen many ministries that minister strictly by faith, and they have a certain amount of results and success, but it isn't God's best.

On the other hand, we have seen people who minister simply by the Holy Spirit. They will not minister by faith to anyone. They exercise the word of knowledge or other gifts of the Spirit, but when the Spirit is not in operation, they will not do a thing. They, too, have a certain amount of success, but it isn't God's best, either.

If you just have the Word, you can dry up. If you just have the Spirit, you can blow up. But if you have both, you will grow up, as someone said. That's why we need both.

We need not only prayer, but the Word. We need not only faith, which comes by hearing the Word; we need to be filled with the Spirit, speaking to ourselves with psalms and hymns and spiritual songs.

Actions Filled With Power

That is when your actions become filled with the power of God. We're going to see the importance of that in the eighth chapter of Acts:

Then Philip went down to the city of Samaria, and preached Christ unto them.

And the people with one accord gave heed unto those things which Philip spake, hearing and seeing the miracles which he did.

For unclean spirits, crying with loud voice, came out of many that were possessed with them: and many taken with palsies, and that were lame, were healed.

And there was great joy in that city.

Acts 8:5-8

Here we see Philip again, this time in full-time ministry as an evangelist. We know he was one of the seven, including Stephen, who were chosen earlier to wait on tables! The apostles had chosen them, laid hands on them, and appointed them as deacons.

Philip went to Samaria and preached Christ, and the people received his message. They saw devils come out of people, crying with a loud voice. Many who were lame and sick with palsy were healed, and the Bible says there was great joy in that city.

A Sorcerer Is Saved

Then the account goes on to tell us there was a man named Simon, a sorcerer who had bewitched the people and had been appointed as a high-ranking spiritualist in the city. The people thought he had the power of God. During the revival, the Bible reports, "Simon also believed."

We also learn that when the church in Jerusalem heard that the Samaritans had received the Word of God, they sent Peter and John to Samaria to minister. The Samaritans had heard and received the Word of God from Philip. Preaching the Gospel, he'd also had tremendous success in healing the sick. And he had baptized the new converts in water.

The Second Blessing

But the Bible says in verses 15 and 16 that Peter and John went to Samaria to pray for them, "that they might receive the Holy Ghost. (For as yet he was fallen upon none of them: only they were baptized in the name of the Lord Jesus.)"

This gives us a clear indication that there is a ministry for the *evangelist* (Philip) and there is a ministry for the *apostle* (Peter and John). The two ministries bring different levels of truth.

Thank God, salvation is not the end; it's just the beginning! We don't have to remain babies. We can grow up in Christ.

Although Samaria had received the Word of God; although they were saved, including the sorcerer; and although they were baptized with water, the Holy Spirit had fallen upon none of them!

God's Best for Me

Here came Peter and John. They prayed for the Samaritans that they would receive the Holy Spirit. That tells me I receive salvation through the hearing of the Word, and then I must receive the baptism with the Holy Spirit as a separate experience.

Those two elements working in my life can produce God's best in me, which is a Christ-like person; a Jesus-kind of believer. This is the kind of believer Jesus described in Mark 16:17, when he said, "These signs shall follow them that believe...."

These signs include, "...in my name shall they cast out devils; they shall speak with new tongues...they shall lay hands on the sick, and they shall recover" (verses 17, 18).

Peter and John prayed for the believers in Samaria, and in Acts 8:18 it says, "And when Simon saw that through laying on of the apostles' hands the Holy Ghost was given, he offered them money."

The Ministry of Impartation

Was Simon saved? Absolutely. Baptized in water? Yes. But he saw *something* in the ministry of the apostles. He saw something in *the ministry of impartation* that he wanted so desperately, he offered money for it.

"Give me also this power, that on whomsoever I lay hands, he may receive the Holy Ghost," Simon asked in verse 19. In other words, he was saying, "Give me the ability of impartation." The ministry of impartation means that the Spirit of God comes into your life in a stronger measure to release in you the giftings God has deposited in you supernaturally.

But Peter thundered:

Thy money perish with thee, because thou hast thought that the gift of God may be purchased with money.

Thou hast neither part nor lot in this matter: for thy heart is not right in the sight of God.

Repent therefore of this thy wickedness, and pray God, if perhaps the thought of thine heart may be forgiven thee.

For I perceive that thou art in the gall of bitterness, and in the bond of iniquity.

Then answered Simon, and said, Pray ye to the Lord for me, that none of these things which ye have spoken come upon me.

Acts 8:20-24

Time for the Apostles

Miracles had been happening through Philip. Devils were cast out through his ministry; sick and crippled people were healed through his ministry; and the city received great joy because of his preaching. But the Holy Spirit had fallen on none of them.

Philip was through ministering. His ministry in Samaria ended with the repentance and salvation of the Samaritans.

However, the apostles Peter and John came now with the gifts and the ability to impart them. When they laid hands on the new believers, the Bible says they were filled with the Holy Spirit.

I believe prophets and apostles have a higher level of impartation capacity. Because they speak prophetically or inspirationally, they can impart to others, strengthening them through the outpouring of the Spirit that is in their ministry.

What Simon Saw

When Simon the former sorcerer saw *that through the laying on of the apostles' hands* the Holy Spirit was given, he offered them money for this power. Simon saw the results of the impartation. The Holy Spirit is invisible. You cannot see the Holy Spirit given, but you can see a *manifestation* when the Spirit is given.

As Paul wrote to the Corinthians, "My speech and my preaching was not with enticing *words* of man's wisdom, but *in demonstration of the Spirit and of power*" (1 Corinthians 2:4).

That means that the ex-sorcerer could not have seen the Holy Spirit as a dove or as a flame of fire; however, he saw that through the ministry of the laying on of hands, the Holy Spirit was given.

No doubt he witnessed people shake, fall under the power, shout, get drunk in the spirit, laugh hysterically, and speak in other tongues. And when he saw that the ministry of the apostle produced an impartation that demonstrated the power of God, he sought it for himself.

The Captivating Anointing

There is something in the Church world that will always captivate those who are seeking power, and that "something" is the anointing. As we see in this account of the Samaritan revival, there is a difference between the anointing for conviction and salvation and the anointing that comes to bless, fill, and equip the saints through the baptism in the Holy Spirit.

I don't know if you've ever been in a service when nearly everyone was drunk in the Spirit, but I've been in many of them. It doesn't happen all the time, but it happens quite regularly where I have congregations drunk in the Spirit, laughing hysterically, down and out on the floor, because the power of God is moving in the form of impartation, in the form of blessing, in the form of filling God's people to overflowing.

What Simon Sought

When Simon saw that, he began to say, "Give me that! Give me that!" If you have the ability to make people happy, joyous, and free — if you have the ability to ease people's burdens because you carry with you a presence and a level of glory that is able to liberate and add to the message of salvation — people will want what you have!

Notice, Simon did not offer Philip the evangelist money, not because the evangelist was inferior — absolutely not — but because what Philip brought to Samaria was the Word of God on salvation. It was just one part of what God had for the people.

Then Peter and John brought the Word of God on the Holy Spirit. And when you put the Word and the Spirit together, there is an explosion, and suddenly Simon said, "Give me that," and he offered money.

Of course, we know Peter was not a diplomat. He told Simon, "Your money perish with you! You're in the gall of bitterness. You're in the bond of iniquity."

Peter's reputation had probably preceded him. No doubt people had heard about Ananias and Sapphira dropping dead. You don't mess with Peter! And the moment Peter started talking to Simon, Simon said, "No, no. I'm not going to pray. *You* pray to the Lord that He would forgive me, that none of the things you said would come upon me!"

Chapter 8
Apostle of Faith

One of the forerunners of ministering in the realm of impartation in modern times was Smith Wigglesworth, the well-known English evangelist.

Wigglesworth is probably most famous for the fact that he reportedly raised 14 people from the dead. Can you imagine that? Some claim he raised more than 20 people from the dead, but, documented, he raised 14 from the dead.

Wigglesworth would move from faith to *special faith*. When you begin to believe the Word of God to the point where you go as far as you can, like Wigglesworth, there will be times when outbursts of supernatural faith will manifest through you.

We were in a certain meeting recently, and a tiny woman came up for prayer. She had pain in her neck and back because of arthritis. I laid my hands on her, but she did not receive. I took my hands off her, and then great faith came on me.

When someone is in pain, you can't grab them and yank them around unless you have received that release into special faith, and you know that what you're about to do is going to work.

I grabbed the woman by the wrists, and when I violently yanked her arms above her head twice, the power of God hit her, and she started to laugh hysterically. She stood there and laughed like a drunk for about 10 minutes, and then fell under the power.

She came back later and told me that not only did the pain leave instantly when I did that, but she had never felt the Spirit of God fall on her as powerfully as it did when I yanked her arms. That was impartation.

Smith Wigglesworth operated in that dimension. He would hit people in the stomach, and tumors would dissolve. When he was criticized for it, he said you cannot be soft with the devil.

Of course, the moment you believe the Bible, you're going to be criticized, because the Bible isn't a book composed of double-talk. The Bible doesn't present a *suggestion;* it presents an absolute method for obeying God. If you don't want criticism, don't believe the Bible.

"I Hit the Devil"

When Wigglesworth was criticized and told, "You hit people. You're too rough," he said, "I don't hit people; I hit the devil. If they get in the way, I can't help it. You can't deal gently with the devil, or comfort him. He likes comfort."

We have also seen tumors dissolve when special faith moved us to hit people. We are learning how to step out of the faith of *the Word* into the manifestation of the faith of *the Spirit.* That is a manifestation of the Holy Spirit: special faith, gifts of healings, and working of miracles.

You can't make it happen when you want to. You can always lay hands on the sick and minister healing to them, and you can always have the anointing working with you, but if you're going to move into a manifestation of the Spirit, it must be sparked or unctioned by Him.

Otherwise, you'll hit someone in the stomach, and you'll hurt them. You'll pull someone out of their wheelchair, and you'll hurt them — because it won't be God doing it through you.

On Raising the Dead

In order to raise the dead, Wigglesworth would approach the situation with as much faith as he had, and then he said he would penetrate heaven with his faith. In other words, he would be seeking a yes answer, and he would be ready.

When Peter raised Tabitha from the dead in Acts 9:36-42, he knelt beside her bed, made everyone leave the room, prayed, and then turned and said to her, "Tabitha, arise!"

What was he doing when he was praying? He was penetrating the throne room of God with great plainness of speech, with his own faith, in order to receive by faith the God-kind of faith. He knew that when he talked to the dead woman, he had to know beyond any doubt that she was going to resurrect.

Preparing To Minister Healing

I remember when I first began to feel the tugging of the Holy Spirit to minister healing to the sick. I began to feel that God wanted me to minister strongly to people with bursitis, arthritis, scoliosis, neck injuries, fused spines, and so forth.

If a man had a crippled arm, I would *almost* be sure that if I grabbed his arm and picked it up, it would be healed. But when I first moved into that realm of ministry, I would stand and hold the person's hand for several minutes; however long it took.

What was I waiting for? I was getting rid of every bit of doubt. You cannot move in faith when you're wondering what is going to happen. You can only move when you know what is going to happen. And you can only know what is going to happen when there is *absolute faith* convincing you of it.

When I settled it in my heart, that's when I moved the hand or arm and the person wouldn't scream — they would be healed and their pain would leave — they were delivered just like that. For months I found myself doing this in a very cautious fashion until I got bolder and stronger in it.

One night we were in a meeting, and everyone who had pain in their body — scoliosis, arthritis, injured shoulders, injured necks — was coming up, and I was yanking them violently, aggressively attacking the condition. People were getting healed one after the other because the gift of special faith was in manifestation.

We've got to move into it. We've got to be convinced of its reality and learn how to cooperate with it, and then we will grow in it. We must start in the beginning by simply ministering to the sick through the conventional means of laying on of hands. And we must find out what God has gifted us with: What kind of manifestations does the Spirit manifest through us?

A Mouthpiece for God

Wigglesworth had special faith working in him. We even call him "the apostle of faith." But I believe with all my heart that Smith Wigglesworth was a prophet. He prophesied important things, and he had several visions. He was a mouthpiece for God in many situations.

He said, "I understand God by His Word. I cannot understand God by impressions or feelings. I cannot get to know God by sentiment. I can only know Him by His Word. It is a dangerous practice to be governed by feelings."

In other words, if Wigglesworth had pain in his body, he didn't go by that pain; he went by Jesus' stripes, and he was healed. This man lived a life of divine health until the day he went to be with the Lord on March 12, 1947. He was 87.

He was attending a funeral and asked a friend how a certain person he had prayed for was doing, and suddenly he was gone. When they inspected his body, the doctor said it was like the body of a young man.

It was common to perform autopsies on the dead in those days, but they didn't do one on Wigglesworth's body, because he had vowed that "no knife will touch this body in life or in death."

When he died, his words were still alive, and the doctors could not perform an autopsy on his body, because he had said it by faith when he was living.

His Faith Was Tested

Of course, his faith was sorely tested. For years Wigglesworth would finish a miracle service and go to his hotel room and roll on the floor in pain from kidney stones. Anyone with less faith than his would have had an operation, but he had made a decision to believe God for his miracle, and he remained adamant, despite the pain.

After six years, he was completely delivered, and he lived in divine health and strength until his late eighties, working hard. He was a good example. He didn't miss God, and he walked in the anointing and the power of the Lord.

It is even said that Wigglesworth grew his third set of teeth. That is awesome! For someone to believe God for a third set of teeth, he would have to have faith!

San Francisco Sees a Miracle

It is also said that when Wigglesworth visited San Francisco years ago, so many people wanted to hear him, he preached and ministered by walking the streets. The people brought out the sick and laid them on mattresses so the shadow of Wigglesworth could pass over them. As it did, the sick were healed. San Francisco witnessed a 20th century Book of Acts miracle.

Why? There was no pretense to Wigglesworth. The reason he had the miracles he had is because he was a man of the Word and of the Spirit. He was a man who believed the Word just like it is, and he was a man who let the Spirit control his life.

Reading in the Holy Ghost

He used to say, "Some people like to read the Bible in the Greek, and some people like to read the Bible in the Hebrew, but I prefer to read my Bible in the Holy Ghost." That's the best way to read the Bible, isn't it? That's when you can get revelation. That's when the Bible lives in you, and you live in it; and in that realm you can ask what you will, and it shall be done unto you.

Wigglesworth used to say, "Faith is an act." A man like that was seldom caught without action. He was a man of action. When he saw something, he took care of it.

One day in his meeting, a demon-possessed man cried with a loud voice and turned around and tried to run out of the building. Wigglesworth ran after him, tackled him, and cast the devil out of him. He was a man of action!

A Man of Action

You see, when the Word and the Spirit are living in you, you are no longer asking a lot of questions or wondering. You become a man of action.

How do you know when you have faith? It is because you can act. You can act before you think! You can detect what the devil is about to do, and you can stop him. If you can't stop him before he does it, you can act while he's in the middle of it and stop him then.

You are a man of immediate action, just like Jesus was when he was walking Jairus to his house and He was stopped by the woman who touched the hem of His garment and was healed. After the interview with this woman, messengers came and told Jairus, "Don't bother the Master any more; your daughter is dead."

Jesus immediately said, "Fear not; only believe." That's a man of action speaking. He did not allow the devil to rob the father of his faith. He immediately counteracted what the devil said with His word — a man of action.

70

A Consistent Man

That is how Wigglesworth was. He used to say, "Faith is an act." He used to say, "Only believe." He is the originator of the phrase, "God said it, I believe it, and that settles it."

There are some dried up, dead, cold, lukewarm, backslidden, powerless theologians running around today who are trying to dispute and argue with some of the things Wigglesworth said.

But anyone who has raised 14 people from the dead is worth listening to. I would rather listen to him than to someone who got his information off a bookshelf and has failed to produce the living faith of God. Faith is an act.

One night Smith Wigglesworth woke up and the devil was in his room. He looked and said, "Oh, it's only you," and he rolled over and went back to sleep. We're talking about a man who had no respect for the devil!

God woke him one night and told him to go to such-and-such a place and raise a person from the dead. He told the Lord, "I'll do it in the morning, Lord," and went back to sleep. He woke up the next morning, put on his clothes, and went over there and raised that person from the dead. That's a man of consistency.

A Visit From Old Man Danube

When Lester Sumrall visited England as a young man, he became well acquainted with Wigglesworth, visiting him in his home and preaching with him. Wigglesworth laid hands on him, wept over him, and prayed that God would release the faith he had in him into Lester Sumrall.

I believe in impartation. I would rather "catch" something from God than have my mind full of information I can't use.

We were with Dr. Sumrall in Sweden and he told of a time he was ministering close to the Danube River, and he called out demon-possessed cases. He said, "If you're here and you're demon possessed, come up here right now," and 300 people began to come out of the congregation!

He said, "No, you don't understand. I said demon possessed." The pastor said, "They know exactly what you said."

And Dr. Sumrall began to command the devil, saying, "By faith in the Name of Jesus Christ of Nazareth, I command you to come out!" People began to writhe like snakes on the floor, and devils began to come out of them.

All of a sudden, a deep, guttural male voice came through a woman and said, "My name is Old Man Danube, and I'll kill her!"

Sumrall replied, "Old Man Danube, my name is Lester Sumrall, and I've come to cast you out!"

Wigglesworth's Impartations

He got that faith because of the impartation Smith Wigglesworth poured into his life through prayer.

Wigglesworth had a presence with him, and he believed in impartation. He believed in sitting next to you and releasing the anointing without saying a word, waiting for the opportunity to witness.

At times, it is reported, people were overwhelmed by the feeling that they were going to die and go to hell — just because they were around him. They would come to him and say, "We don't understand what it is about you, but your presence makes us feel as if we're going to die and go to hell. Would you pray for us?" You can't do that without an anointing being with you, accompanying you wherever you go.

You need the Word and the Spirit to ignite the power of the living God like this.

Faith by Association

Once when Dr. Sumrall was in Java, he was awakened in the middle of the night by a demonic manifestation which was walking his bed across the room. He woke up and told the devil, "Put it back!" He didn't say, "Stop it," or "Knock it off." He said, "Put it back!" And he made the devil that walked his bed across the room walk it back where it belonged!

He got that faith through impartation — through association — with Smith Wigglesworth. There are certain things you glean by association with the right crowd, and there are certain things you glean by impartation from the right crowd.

We know this is biblical, because when the disciples performed the miracles they did, it was because Jesus had said, "You will receive the same Spirit I have. I will ask the Father, and He will send you the Holy Spirit."

When the religious people saw the disciples performing miracles, it was obvious they had been with Jesus. They had associated with Him — they had received an impartation from Him — and they had become like Him in ministry.

A Fearless Stance

Wigglesworth said, "God said it, I believe it, and that settles it." If you believe what God said, that settles it in your life, and no devil can rob you of what God has promised you.

Wigglesworth also said, "Fear looks; faith jumps." Fear is always wondering, "What are we going to do?" Faith has no time to hesitate, and faith does not respond or react to the devil. Faith always acts from a position of superiority to the devil. We see that in the life of Jesus. We always see Jesus taking command. We always see the disciples taking command because of the power they had through the Holy Spirit.

Wigglesworth used to say, "Any man can be changed by faith." That includes all of us. He would say, "Never say 'I can't' if you're filled with the Holy Ghost." People say, "I can't" all the time, but all things are possible to him that believes. So if you are filled with the Holy Spirit, never say "I can't," because you *can* do all things.

Chapter 9
The Emergence of the Third Move

Oral Roberts said he and his fellow healing evangelists owe Smith Wigglesworth a debt beyond calculation. Why? I believe Wigglesworth was a forerunner of a balanced message, saying there is the Word and there is the Spirit, and when they are combined, a mighty revival will result.

Wigglesworth prophesied, "There is coming a move that will restore the gifts of the Spirit. Then there will come a second move that will emphasize the Word."

Then he prophesied, "When these two moves of the Spirit combine, we will see the greatest move the Church of Jesus Christ has ever seen. I won't see it, but it is going to come, and it is going to be greater in its dimension of the miraculous and success in God than anything any of us have ever encountered."

The Gifts Restored

As you know, the restoration of the gifts of the Holy Spirit took place during the Healing Revival of the 1950s. After Wigglesworth and Aimee Semple McPherson died, a mighty healing revival swept this nation.

The media by and large chose to ignore it, but people by the millions came to the saving knowledge of Jesus Christ during the Healing Revival, when great men of God like Jack Coe, William Branham, A. A. Allen, Oral Roberts, and many others were on the scene ministering powerfully.

75

The blind were seeing, the deaf were hearing, the lame were leaping for joy, and it brought the Church a new revelation of the gifts of the Spirit and the knowledge that there were men and women who still operate in the gifts of healings and still have the working of miracles in their life.

The Healing Revival Didn't Die

Many believe the Healing Revival ended, but I don't believe it died; I believe the healing evangelists died. I don't believe it is God's best for us to wait for a future date for miracles.

This is the day the Lord has made; I will rejoice and be glad in it. We can have miracles *today*. Jesus Christ is the same *today* as He was yesterday.

But to have miracles, we are going to have to pay the price. The great men and women of faith in the past paid the price, and part of the price was in their thought life. They weren't liberal thinkers; they were people of absolutes. They chose the best route and made it the only route.

The Charismatic Movement Emerges

During the time the Healing Revival died down because the evangelists had left the forefront, there came in the 1960s the Charismatic Movement and a woman by the name of Kathryn Kuhlman. Kathryn Kuhlman rarely ministered to the sick by faith. What she did was open the eyes of the Church. She brought a fresh awareness regarding the person and gifts of the Holy Spirit.

By worship and praise, and by turning the hearts of the people to the Lord, the tangible presence of the Spirit released the revelation gifts — the word of knowledge and the word of wisdom. Miss Kuhlman operated in the gifts, and people were healed.

They were also healed through *the corporate prayer of faith,* which normally does not involve the laying on of hands.

Wigglesworth foresaw the Charismatic Movement when he was alive. This movement began to reach beyond denominational barriers, and it brought a revelation of the Person of the Holy Spirit to the Church. People started getting saved in all kinds of denominations. Catholics started getting baptized with the Holy Spirit.

The Word/Faith Movement Arrives

Shortly after the Charismatic Movement emerged, there came a revelation known as the Word/Faith Movement. Some people act as if it never happened. I don't care what the skeptics say; the Word/Faith Movement is a genuine, sound, Bible-based foundation for the Church. Without the revelation of the integrity of the Word of God, a Christian is powerless against his adversary.

Here came men and women who began to preach about the integrity of God's Word and His promises. One such man was Kenneth E. Hagin, who at the time of the Healing Revival was preaching and teaching in churches.

He didn't have a tent, and he wasn't a famous preacher, but he was on the scene. When the Charismatic Movement came, it was a launching pad for him to join in and bring the message of the Word: "You can have what you say."

Critics may call it the "Blab it and grab it" or "Name it and claim it" move, but the Bible is clear: "What things soever ye desire, when ye pray, believe that ye receive them, and ye shall have them" (Mark 11:24).

When we believe in the integrity of God's Word, we don't need the gifts to be in operation, or we don't need to feel goose bumps, or we don't need a certain atmosphere to be present in order to receive answers from God.

The Era of the Teacher

The Word/Faith Movement was the era of the teacher, just as the Healing Revival had been the era of the evangelist. The Lord brought a strong emphasis on the Word and faith through Kenneth E. Hagin, Kenneth Copeland, and many other faith teachers.

It may have seemed like the evangelist went out and the teacher came in, but God never fights against Himself. When He anoints the evangelist and then brings in the teacher, it's only because the teacher can add to what the evangelist did. It's not to separate or divide the two, but to put them together and come up with a great and mighty weapon to use to defeat the works of the devil.

There came the revelation, "I don't go by what I feel; I believe what the Bible says. It doesn't matter what the symptoms are; I quote the Word.

"It doesn't matter what my financial condition is; my God shall supply all of my need according to His riches in glory. It doesn't matter if I feel weak; let the weak say, 'I am strong.' Be strong in the Lord and in the power of His might. Resist the devil, and he will flee from you."

This revelation of the integrity of the Word and the authority of the believer came through the Word/Faith Movement.

The Third Move That's Coming

But Wigglesworth didn't stop here. While he was still alive, he prophesied of a third move. He said, "In that third move, the Church is going to take the gifts of the Spirit; its awareness of the Third Person of the Trinity; its awareness of the revelation gifts, the utterance gifts, and the power gifts; and it's going to put it together with a balance: the Word-based revelation of the integrity of God."

Wigglesworth concluded, "It's going to be the most powerful move the world has ever known."

Do you realize it belongs to you and me?

Bulldog Faith

Wigglesworth was a man of tenacious faith. However, he never expected others to adhere to a standard he was not willing to live himself.

One day they brought a crippled child to him. The Spirit of the Lord moved him, and he literally kicked the child off the platform! As the crowd gasped, the child just flew through the air — and when he landed, he was completely healed!

A human mind cannot understand that. We can never hope to get to that dimension in faith unless we begin to believe God in the little things and become like a bulldog. We must hold onto God's promises and not allow men's opinions, theology, doctrine, religiosity, or traditions rob us of what we believe God has for us.

The Day Polly Died

While Wigglesworth was away from home one day holding a meeting, his wife, Polly, died. When he got home, he resurrected her from the dead and tried to talk her out of leaving this life! She said, "I want to go to be with the Lord. It's my time to go."

Can you imagine: You die, but you can't get rid of your husband! His faith wouldn't quit, and he raised her from the dead. She had to convince him that it was time for her to go. Otherwise, she couldn't have gone, because his faith would have held her here.

I know that doesn't sit right with the religious mind, because we think that when your number comes up, it's your time. But the Bible says, "With long life will I satisfy him, and shew him my salvation" (Psalm 91:16).

Wigglesworth was so bold, many of the preachers around him tended to believe him even when he was joking. You can get so bold in God, and people can see you have so many results, that your words will carry great weight.

Living in Psalm 91

A man once came to Wigglesworth and said, "How dare you say you are going to live to such-and-such age when the

Bible says it's threescore and ten, and you are already beyond that?"

Wigglesworth responded, "Where does it say that?"

The man answered, "In the 90th Psalm."

Wigglesworth said, "I don't live in the 90th Psalm; I live in the 91st Psalm. It says, 'With long life will I satisfy him, and show him my salvation.'"

Then one day as he was sitting at the dinner table, he told some friends, "I just found out in Genesis that man's days shall be 120. I think I'll live to be 120."

Someone said, "Now we know how long you'll live. If you live to be 120, that will be the end of your days."

Wigglesworth replied, "Well, if I get to be somewhere around there and I'm not satisfied, I'll just jump over to the 91st Psalm again."

Believing for God's Best

Now we laugh about it and say, "Well, it didn't happen. He died at age 87." Yes, but he died at 87 healing the sick. He died at 87 raising the dead. He died at 87 with his bills paid, the devil under his feet, and God exalted in his life.

The reason was not because God sovereignly chose to give Smith Wigglesworth a different lifestyle of victory. No, it was because he *contended* for the faith, *believed* for it, and *expected* great things to happen, believing for God's best.

Wigglesworth saw some of the most powerful things man could see, yet he prophesied that even *greater* things would come to our generation.

Wigglesworth gave the torch to others who were in contact with him, and now they are running with it.

Chapter 10
Imparting Strong Faith

During the Healing Revival, generally dated by historians as 1947 to 1958, literally hundreds of ministries were involved in healing the sick and casting out devils.

It was a tremendous move of God! The healing evangelists were waging a tenacious battle against sickness and disease. People were getting healed by the thousands, and the Church was also having great success in getting people delivered from alcohol, drugs, and tobacco.

Today, some of those evangelists would be considered people who "hype" and go to extremes to get the crowd into a high vein of enthusiasm and excitement. But regardless of what people think, genuine miracles took place in their services night after night.

Fortunately, we can still witness some of the meetings of William Branham, A. A. Allen, and Jack Coe today, because they were filmed. We see up to 90 persons who were bedfast or confined to a wheelchair get up healed in the middle of a strong move of God.

There was such boldness and such a strong conviction that Jesus Christ is the same today as He was yesterday, people were almost afraid *not* to be healed.

The evangelists were so strong in their message, most of them said, "If you don't get healed, it's because you don't have faith." Although that is not a popular message today, there is a lot of truth in it.

Strong Faith

However, it isn't our desire to condemn people, or make them feel guilty because they don't have strong faith. It's our job to impart strong faith to them. If they don't get it immediately, we can still work with them. We must learn to hate the devil. We must learn to hate sickness. But we must learn to love people.

There is a balance, an accuracy, there. There is a truth in being strong about what you are preaching. Sometimes you've got to be rough with people if you're going to help them. Otherwise, you might get on their good side and end up burying them. I'd rather get on their *bad* side and see them get healed!

The healing evangelists were rough. Jack Coe had strong faith and was rough. He would walk down the healing line, pick people out of wheelchairs — and let go of them. If they fell, they fell. And if they stood, they stood. By and large, 60 to 70 percent of those he picked up out of their wheelchairs were healed instantly and walked off. That's a pretty good percentage!

Kathryn Kuhlman

Out of that driving, enthusiastic, high-energy Healing Movement came the Charismatic Movement — and Kathryn Kuhlman. Miss Kuhlman was a woman of the Spirit, but she did not agree with a lot of the methods the healing evangelists used.

I believe there are two viewpoints regarding healing. The one espoused by the healing evangelists was, "We will believe God by faith; and we will push, press in, and agree together — and we will see it happen."

On the other side was the Charismatic viewpoint held by Kathryn Kuhlman and others, who said, "We will just worship the Lord, and we will let the Spirit of the Lord bring the miracle. If you get healed, God healed you. If you don't get healed, we don't understand why some people are healed and others aren't."

Both Viewpoints Needed

The reason I am mentioning these viewpoints is because we need both today. The Lord told me we need to have the Charismatics' love of worship, praise, atmosphere, the power of God falling, and people getting healed as well as the healing evangelists' preference for the gifts of the Spirit in operation. We also need tenacity when there is no anointing or flow in a meeting to blast through the hindrance and let the flow of God come.

God never eclipsed the Healing Revival by the Charismatic Movement! Neither did He eclipse the Charismatic Movement by the Word/Faith Movement. His intention was for us to take *everything* that is biblical in all these moves and combine it so we could see the full picture of what God is doing in the earth today.

We have been studying about prophets and the miracle ministry of the prophet. One reason for our study is because prophets tell you what's coming. We have learned through the Word and through the mouth of Jesus and other messengers that a revival is coming. This coming move of God will be stronger than anything we've experienced before.

William Branham

William Branham was a modern prophet. He became a controversial man later in his ministry, but he was a man of the Spirit — a man of extraordinary visions and revelations. He was what I call a *seer*. He was like an Old Testament prophet. There is no doubt that he had the gift of God working in him.

The angel of the Lord that had talked to him since childhood appeared to him on May 7, 1946 and told him, "Fear not. I am sent from the presence of Almighty God to tell you that...God has sent you to take a gift of divine healing to the people of the world." The angel also told Branham he would be able to detect and diagnose all diseases and afflictions when the gift was operating.

Looking Over the Wall

Branham saw events before they took place. He used to look into people's lives by the Spirit. The late Demos Shakarian told me that when he asked Brother Branham, "How do you do it?" Branham said it was almost as if he pulled himself over a wall through his faith and looked into people's lives.

It was not unusual for people to come on the platform and for Brother Branham to give their name and address, diagnose their condition, tell them how long they'd been in that condition, name the doctor they'd been seeing, and repeat what the doctor had said. Then, after he had confirmed that everything he had said was true, he would tell them to go home and believe God, because they were healed.

Equipping the Saints

The Bible tells us that the ministry gifts (apostle, prophet, evangelist, pastor, and teacher) and the gifts of the Spirit, such as the word of knowledge, are alive and active today. They are going to be part of equipping the saints for the work of the ministry, so we can work together to bring about this great and mighty harvest that God intends to give.

It is said that William Branham was in a meeting one night when a man wearing dark glasses was escorted into the building, as if he were blind, by two other men.

Branham stopped in the middle of his sermon and said, "Three men just walked into the building. The one in the middle is faking blindness. Two men are walking you down the aisle. You have come here to mock the man of God, but you are going to be blind for a season."

Everyone in the congregation heard the man scream in horror as his eyes literally went blind as the prophet spoke the Word of the Lord.

I believe God is calling us in this hour to believe the Word and to flow in the Spirit that strongly. Then, every time the devil tries to do something against us, it will turn around and become an embarrassment to him, because the Church of Jesus Christ has been born into the kingdom. This generation has been born into the kingdom for such an hour as this. God has called us to live like this.

The Boy in the Vision

One day Branham saw a vision of a boy who was hit by a car. He was lying by the side of a road. His clothing was rumpled and he was fatally injured. Branham knew he would raise him from the dead. From that time on, he shared this vision and told people all over the country to write the prediction in their Bibles, because it would surely come to pass.

One day they brought Branham to a boy who had drowned, but when the prophet looked at him, he said, "No, that's not the one I saw in the vision."

Later, as he was riding through Finland, he saw a crowd gathered by the side of the road. He asked the driver to stop. When he got out of the car and investigated, it was the same boy he had seen in the vision — and he raised that boy from the dead!

Things like that happened to Branham continually. He didn't operate without the gifts. He would have visions and then come to the meeting, and when people would come for prayer, they were the same people he had seen in the vision. He could diagnose their conditions better than any doctor could. And he could provide the answers they needed for their conditions.

A Ministry With Mystique

Actually, Branham's ministry had a lot of mystique about it, because anytime a man operates so strongly in a gift, people tend to gravitate toward him and believe that everything he says is straight from God.

I believe we must be sure as Christians that we are not only people of the Spirit, but we are people of the Word. Why? Because in this day and age, we cannot afford to see any more ministries rise and fall. We need to see them make it all the way through.

There is a biblical standard for success in the ministry, and I will give you an example of it. During the Healing Revival, Brother Hagin was brushing shoulders with all these evangelists. He was not as popular as they were. He didn't buy a tent, although many people prophesied over him that he should. He remained in local churches and ministered in the level of grace he felt God had given him.

Building on the Word

But he used to tell many of those evangelists, "When you're gone, I'll still be around, because you're building on a gift, and I'm building on the Word of God."

Before William Branham died on Christmas Eve 1965, Gordon Lindsay, Brother Hagin, and several others knew by revelation of the Holy Spirit that Branham was going to die. Brother Hagin knew that Branham would die unless he stopped trying to be a teacher of the Word and stayed within the higher level of anointing God had given him as a prophet.

The message was delivered to Branham, but he said, "I know I'm not called to teach, but I like to teach, so I'm going to continue doing it."

Even though he could call you by name, detect your condition, and bring a cure to you, he was lacking in the area of doctrine and the Word! What happened was, the devil used that weakness in him to cause him to stumble.

But just because it happened does not lessen his success; nor should we throw away the gift he had. We need that gift. We need it alive in the church today. We need it alongside the Word of God so whoever flows in it can continue to maintain a long and successful ministry; and when they don't have a supernatural gift, they will still have the Word, and vice versa.

Supernatural Signs

Branham had two supernatural signs that were peculiar to his ministry: pulsations and swelling in his left hand and the operation of the word of knowledge.

When he took the left hand of a sick person, he would feel vibrations in his own left hand which would allow him to discern which diseases the person was suffering from.

If demonic activity was present, his hand would swell and become red, and it would be visible to everyone. When the demon spirit came into contact with the gift of God, Branham would feel like he had grabbed an electric line. In fact, the impact was so strong, his watch would stop. Then, when he would cast the oppressing spirit out, the swelling would go down, and his hand would return to normal.

By the way, when the prophet was flowing in the gift, 100 percent of the people would be healed miraculously by the power of God!

Sometimes Branham would push away the microphone and tell a person privately, "In order for God to heal you, you need to repent of this hidden sin that is going on in your life." No one else heard their whispered conversation. When the person repented, God healed and delivered him.

God's Will Is To Heal Everyone

When we regard a gift like Branham's and see that God is willing to call people by name and minister healing to them, we can understand how it is God's will to heal everyone.

Some people think it *isn't* God's will to heal everyone, because not everyone gets healed. But if that were the case, it isn't God's will to *save* everybody, because not everyone gets saved. Nevertheless, it *is* God's will to bless His people; to give them the healing blessings of Calvary through a ministry gift.

Sometimes we can't see the full picture. We don't know, for example, if unconfessed sin is involved in someone's sickness. We don't know if there is a lack of faith on the person's part. Or we don't know if the minister lacks guidance from the Holy Spirit to detect what kind of condition the person has and what its root cause is.

Despite that, we must press in and believe for 100 percent results, even when we only see 30 to 60 percent results. We must believe for one hundred percent results every time we step into the arena of divine healing!

The Word of Knowledge Builds Faith

The second sign Branham had that helped elevate the faith of the people to a place where they could receive healing was the gift of the word of knowledge. Because this gift is ministered to *individuals*, not corporately, it is impossible to minister this way to a congregation made up of hundreds or thousands of people. However, once 10, 20, or 30 people were individually ministered to by the gift of the word of knowledge, the faith of the whole congregation would rise to a place where they could receive the prayer of faith that went through Branham, and miracles would happen.

Chapter 11
The Realm of Perception

A nd there sat a certain man at Lystra, impotent in his feet,
being a cripple from his mother's womb, who never
had walked:

The same heard Paul speak: who stedfastly beholding
him, and *perceiving* that he had faith to be healed,

Said with a loud voice, Stand upright on thy feet. And he
leaped and walked.

Acts 14:8-10

This was a form of the word of knowledge. *I believe that
perception is a form of the word of knowledge.*

You know it is impossible to see whether someone has
faith or not, because you can't "see" faith with your natural
eye. It must be *spiritually discerned.*

When we are ministering, there are things we know
when we're in the anointing that we think we know because
we're so smart, but that's not it at all. We look at someone,
and the Lord talks to us about them. We know by the Holy
Spirit because the anointing is there. If that anointing is
removed, you know a great deal less.

I can look at people at times and the Lord will show me
things about them. I'll know what they are saying in their
heart to the Lord. I'll know when they are saying, "I wish I
could believe." And I'll know when they say, "I believe."
This is because there is *a realm of perception* that you can tune
into in God when the Holy Spirit has anointed you.

We learned earlier that Paul was a prophet at Antioch even before he was released to operate as an apostle. There is a realm of perception that operates in the revelation realm.

Exploding Into the Faith Dimension

Do you know the Bible says, "ye may all prophesy one by one, that all may learn, and all may be comforted" (1 Corinthians 14:31). So when that anointing is there, the children of God can prophesy a measure of the Gospel — can prophesy by faith what the scripture says — and it will not be a manifestation of their mind, will, or emotions. It will indeed be a manifestation of the Holy Ghost, and it will carry with it life that will sometimes explode a congregation into a dimension of faith!

The Bible says that when a sinner comes into our midst and hears us prophesy, "the secrets of his heart" are exposed "and falling down on his face he will worship God, and report that God is in you of a truth" (1 Corinthians 14:24). Why? Because you have "read his mail," so to speak.

That's how witnessing works, too. You don't witness just by handing out tracts; you witness by detecting where that person is spiritually.

If someone comes to your home or place of business, and you offer him something he doesn't want, he's not going to accept it. The same holds true with someone who is lost. You must know where he's at in order to "hook" him and make him want to receive what you have.

Paul Perceived Faith

So Paul, the Bible says, perceiving by the Holy Spirit that the crippled man had faith to be healed, zeroed in. Probably there were many people there that day who needed a miracle and many whom God was willing to heal. But there was a connection between Paul and this man who had never walked.

Paul got hold of him in the spirit and detected he had faith. Again, it was a form of the word of knowledge. Acts 14:9 and 10 says that Paul "stedfastly beholding him...said with a loud voice...."

Sometimes we need a *loud* voice! Sometimes if we're not ready to say it in a loud voice, we're not ready to experience it. Sometimes a loud voice is the by-product of big faith — not always, but sometimes.

When you're saying to a crippled man who has never walked, out loud in front of a crowd, "Stand upright on your feet!" it's because you know that you know that you know that power is going to go out of your word, be received by him, and he's going to respond.

We see in Acts 3:6 where Peter at the Gate Beautiful told that other crippled man, "In the name of Jesus Christ of Nazareth rise up and walk." But then he had to take him by the hand and yank him up in order to help the impartation take place. There is commitment, strength, and involvement in that realm of perception.

So Paul perceived and William Branham perceived. Branham operated in that realm by pulling himself over a wall, as it were, and began to see into people's lives.

Combining the Spirit and the Word

The Charismatic Movement in the sixties opened our eyes to the gifts of the Holy Spirit. Now the third wave of bringing the Word and the Spirit together is coming. We need to operate with the Spirit and the Word combined.

We were in South Africa recently in a time of impartation, and the gifts of revelation began to operate. Robin looked at a certain woman and said, "There is one thing in your life that you cannot believe God for. You can believe God for everything else but this one thing."

The next day the woman brought her 10-year-old son who had been born dumb. He had never spoken a word. As she brought him up to the altar she was already teary-eyed, because that word was so real to her. Until that time she had probably believed that God *can* heal, but that belief didn't do her any good.

Just because God *can* heal does not mean He *will*. It takes our will to believe that He will in order to receive His goodness.

A Time Not To Pray

When the mother brought the boy to the altar for me to pray for him, I knew in my spirit that I shouldn't pray for him. Instead, I bent down, looked at him, and said, "Do you know who I am?" He *said*, "Man."

I said, "Man of God." He *said*, "Man of God."

I said, "Jesus is healing you, isn't he?" He *said*, "Jesus is healing me."

I said, "Say, 'Hallelujah.'" He *said*, "Hallelujah."

I said, "Say, 'Praise the Lord.'" He *said*, "Praise the Lord!"

The congregation went wild! The mother went wild. People were shouting and clapping and glorifying God.

It was a *perception* in me that *the healing was already done*, simply by the act of the mother bringing the child for prayer. It was done in the spirit. Sometimes things are done in the spirit realm and we don't know it.

Knowing by the Inward Witness

An Indian woman came to my meeting. She wasn't even saved. She had a blood clot in her left leg, and she was carried to the altar. She didn't know a thing about ministry.

When I laid my hands on her, she fell under the power. After a while, they helped her to her feet, but she still held her left leg as if it were still crooked. She still appeared to be sick.

I said, "I want you to stand on the left leg and pick the right leg up." I said that because I knew what had happened. Sometimes you just know by an inward witness in your spirit that it's time to stop praying, it's time to stop asking, because it's over — it's done. When this woman stood on her left leg, it dawned on her that she was healed.

I was in a meeting in Northern California one day, and a woman in tormenting pain came up for prayer. Her back was deteriorating. I said, "Turn around and show me where it is."

When I said that, the pastor knew I was going to hit her in the back. His wife knew I was going to hit her in the back. And my wife knew I was going to hit her in the back.

"Don't Hit Her in the Back!"

Later, the pastor told me, "I almost stopped you and said, 'Don't hit her in the back! She's in a lot of pain.'" But before he could talk me out of it, I had hit her in the back, and she was completely healed by the power of God! Why? Because there is a "knowing" that can operate in you.

When we were in Florida recently, eight deaf people received their healing in one service. The eighth person I prayed for had been born without an eardrum. When I put my finger in her left ear, it felt as big around as a quarter. I pulled my finger back out and put my hand over her ear.

I said, "How many of you believe this woman is going to hear out of an ear that does not have an eardrum?" The natural mind, you see, cannot receive the things of the Spirit of God; they are foolishness to him. He cannot know them.

That woman started hearing perfectly. She plugged up her right ear and was hearing perfectly out of her left ear — the ear that did not have an eardrum in it. This is what God wants for us today.

The Gift Does Not Do Away With the Word

When we were in Taos, New Mexico, several years ago, a man in the service had been believing God for healing, standing on the verse in First Peter 2:24, "By whose stripes ye were healed." Standing on God's Word is a valid thing to do.

But that night I had a word of knowledge. I said, "Someone is here with a left shoulder that is in bad shape. You have a lot of pain. God wants to heal your left shoulder."

The man didn't come forward. He was in the back of the congregation, thinking, "Well, I'm already healed by Jesus' stripes. I'm standing on the Word. I don't know if I should go up there, because by going up, I might be denying my miracle."

But the gift does not do away with the Word, and the Word does not do away with the gift. They work together. Because that man was believing he was healed, God gave me a word of knowledge to make that manifestation a reality.

A Creative Miracle

I had a further word. I said, "You're standing by faith. You believe by His stripes you were healed. Come up here." And the man came. He had a short-sleeved shirt on, and his shoulder was visible. The left shoulder protruded up like a pyramid.

He had fallen off a cliff and had broken the shoulder. It did not heal right. They were getting ready to break the shoulder cap, insert an artificial one, and reset his arm.

When I laid my hands on him, he fell under the power. The power of God was on him. That deformed shoulder was moving independent of his arm as fast as a piston would move in an engine. It was going b-b-b-b-b-b-b-b.

I said, "Look at that!" and as many people as could crowd around him watched as this man's bone moved independently of the rest of his arm. After he had lain there a while, he stood up, and now he could move his arm and shoulder with ease. He had no pain. He was completely delivered instantly.

It was a creative miracle that was brought about through the gift of the word of knowledge. This is a documented healing.

There are no limits on God. The limits are at our end. When we receive something from God, we can keep it, we can run with it, and we can allow it to be a blessing in our life.

Chapter 12
Our Destiny: Giant Killers!

Now I want to share with you what I believe is our destiny.

In this book, although we started in the Book of Acts, we have spanned about a hundred years of recent Church history.

We have studied the champions of faith — the children of destiny — in the past century to validate and demonstrate that there is a pattern to be found in the moves of God.

These moves led people out of the Dark Ages, out of the Reformation, and out of the simple evangelical or salvation message into the place where divine healing, prosperity, the integrity of the Word, the validity of the gifts of the Holy Spirit, and the restoration of the ministry gifts are viable.

We spanned all this to come to our conclusion: What is the Body of Christ facing today?

A Visitation

Several years ago while my wife, Robin, and I were lying in bed, resting, she had a vision that answers this question.

We weren't speaking about anything spiritual. I had my hand on her stomach, and all of a sudden we grew silent. We began to sense the witness of the Holy Spirit in our hearts that something was about to happen.

I felt a slight surge of anointing leave my hand and enter into Robin's body. When it did, we began to feel the presence of the Lord move into the room. The stronger the presence got, the stronger the surge coming out of my right hand became. I have never felt quite the same release of anointing come out of my body.

The power of God pinned Robin to the bed, and the glory of God filled the room. We both remained silent. This experience lasted 12 to 15 minutes.

A Giant With Nail Prints

Robin saw a vision of a giant with nail prints in his hands and feet, with fire coming out of his eyes, a sword coming out of his mouth, and light coming out of his hands.

This giant was standing, planted firmly on top of a seven-headed dragon that had seven different faces. Demons were running in terror in every direction around the head of the giant, and there were chariots of fire with angelic beings in them.

When Robin came to, the surge of power in my hand began diminishing, and the glory cloud started leaving. Afterwards we remained silent a few more minutes before we were able to speak.

The Interpretation

Robin described the vision to me, and the Spirit of the Lord spoke to me and gave me the interpretation, saying:

"That giant is the Body of Christ; the Church of Jesus Christ. I will build my Church, and the gates of hell will not prevail against it. Jesus Christ is the Head. The Church is the Body.

"The reason it has nail prints in its hands and feet is because it has been crucified with Christ. Nevertheless, it lives, yet not it, but it is Christ who is living in it.

"The reason it has fire coming out of its eyes is because the Church will have discernment, loving righteousness and hating iniquity. It will know what is of God. It will know what is of the devil. It will believe God and resist the devil.

"The reason it has a sword coming out of its mouth is because the Church is going to speak and believe the Word.

And like a two-edged sword, it will pierce to bring the power of God to a world that lies in darkness.

"The reason it has shafts of light coming out of its hands is because the healing power of God has been given to the Church to operate. Behold, I give you power over all the power of the devil, and nothing shall by any means hurt you.

"And the reason it is standing on top of a seven-headed dragon is because all the power of the devil is going to be subdued spiritually by the Church of Jesus Christ!"

The Bible says of Jesus:

Wherefore God also hath highly exalted him, and given him a name which is above every name:

That *at the name of Jesus every knee should bow*, of things in heaven, and things in earth, and things under the earth.

Philippians 2:9,10

Cancer, AIDS Will Bow the Knee!

That means while we're here on earth, we're going to see cancer bow the knee to the Name of Jesus Christ; AIDS bow the knee to the Name of Jesus Christ; every other incurable condition, bondage, and demon spirit that holds men bound (if they are willing to be set free); and every demonic force, disease, affliction, infirmity, and hopeless condition bow the knee to the Name of Jesus Christ!

The reason the dragon had seven different faces is because Satan will utilize everything within his power to solicit his evil. If he cannot get you involved in Satanism, he'll try to get you involved in Christian Science, Mormonism, or spiritualism. And there are presently Christians calling 1-900 numbers to get a word from a psychic!

If the devil cannot get you to walk out on God, he'll try to do the second, third, fourth, or tenth best thing. That's why he has different faces. He cannot appear to everyone as a hideous creature. He tries to transform himself into an angel of light.

We know that the vision we had is real, because the Bible says in Ephesians 4:11-13:

And he gave some, apostles; and some, prophets; and some, evangelists; and some, pastors and teachers;

For the perfecting of the saints, for the work of the ministry, for the edifying of the body of Christ:

Till we all come in the unity of the faith, and of the knowledge of the Son of God, unto a perfect man, unto the measure of the stature of the fullness of Christ.

That "perfect man" sounds like a giant, doesn't he?

The Bible says of Jesus:

And [God] hath put all things under his feet, and gave him to be the head over all things to the church,

Which is his body, the fullness of him that filleth all in all.

Ephesians 1:22,23

Here we are, entrusted with the most powerful dispensation in history!

Go After the Devil!

We can believe the Word, pray and be filled with the Spirit, and keep ourselves from the wicked one. And instead of "holding the fort," we can go after the devil's fort, pull down his fortresses, take land from him, and take souls for the glory of the kingdom of God.

Greater is He that is in us than he that is in the world!

Other books by Dr. Christian Harfouche

Authority Over the Powers of Darkness
Doing the Impossible
How To Receive Your Miracle
Living On The Cutting Edge
The Hidden Power of Your Words
The Silver, The Gold, and The Glory
The Spirit Guide

For orders or more information contact:

Christian Harfouche Ministries
4317 N. Palafox St
Pensacola, FL. 32505
www.globalrevival.com

Or visit our website:
www.globalrevival.com